RESTORING
THE
APOSTOLIC FAITH

A History of the Early Pentecostal Movement

Foreword by David K. Bernard

RESTORING
THE
APOSTOLIC FAITH

A History of the Early Pentecostal Movement

J. L. Hall

WORD AFLAME PRESS

Restoring the Apostolic Faith

by J. L. Hall

©2007 Word Aflame Press
Hazelwood, MO 63042-2299

ISBN 978-1-56722-702-4

Cover Design by Laura Jurek

All Scripture quotations in this book are from the King James Version of the Bible unless otherwise identified.

Illustrations reproduced on the following pages are used by the permission of Flower Pentecostal Heritage Center: 21, 28, 53, 61, 103, 134, 142, 150.

Printed in United States of America

Printed by

WORD AFLAME PRESS
8855 Dunn Road, Hazelwood, MO 63042
www.pentecostalpublishing.com

CONTENTS

FOREWORD

By David K. Bernard

Over the past forty years, J. L. Hall has been a leader in the United Pentecostal Church International. He has well served the apostolic movement as a teacher, preacher, editor, writer, theologian, and historian.

During his tenure as editor in chief, the *Pentecostal Herald* proclaimed the apostolic message worldwide, and the *Forward* provided valuable resources for ministers. The selection of Word Aflame Press books grew from a mere handful to over 150 in print on a variety of biblical, ministerial, and practical subjects. He actively supervised the approval and editing of all periodicals, tracts, books, and Sunday school literature. He was also instrumental in organizing the first Oneness Pentecostal symposiums, overseeing the Historical Center (now the Center for the Study of Oneness Pentecostalism), formulating the Judicial Procedure, and chairing the Parliamentary Committee.

As an editor, he guided authors toward an effective, well-reasoned, biblical presentation of their message. It was my good fortune that he edited most of the articles and books that I have written. As a writer, he is best known for his articles on Pentecostal doctrine and history, many of which form the basis of this book.

J. L. Hall is widely respected both inside and outside the Oneness Pentecostal movement as one of its foremost theologians and historians. He contributed several articles for *The New International Dictionary of the Pentecostal and Charismatic Movements* (2002), including the one on the UPCI, and is the only living Oneness leader to be the subject of an article in it. Often he has played a key role in dealing with theological issues, constitutional and judicial matters, and difficult decisions in our movement. Leaders have valued his advice as sound, unbiased, and uninfluenced by personal agendas. He is a kind, gracious, steadfast, and articulate spokesman for the apostolic faith.

This present volume unfolds J. L. Hall's understanding of the historical development of the Pentecostal movement and the Oneness Pentecostal movement in particular. He sees the restoration impulse—the desire to restore the church to its apostolic roots—as the best lens through which to understand Oneness Pentecostalism. This book is a valuable addition to the growing body of literature devoted to understanding modern Pentecostalism.

CONTENDING FOR THE FAITH

With an eye toward his day and the future of the church, Jude wrote that we are to "earnestly contend for the faith which was once delivered unto the saints" (Jude 3). Through the centuries, the power of this exhortation has echoed in the ears of those who have sought to discover again the experience, doctrine, and ministry of the early apostolic church.

The Falling Away

Jude wrote his epistle around AD 65, only one generation after the Day of Pentecost. It may surprise us that at this early date the church was already struggling against false doctrines, but like weeds, erroneous teachings spring up quickly. Jude was not the only voice warning against false teachers and their corrupt doctrines. Similar warnings are found in many other epistles, including those written by the apostles Paul, Peter, and John. For example, Paul wrote prophetically of a "falling away" in the church before the return of Jesus Christ (II Thessalonians 2:3).

Signs of this falling away were visible when Jude wrote his epistle, and early church history reveals that by the end of the fourth century the falling away from the "faith which was once delivered unto the saints" had become a visible corporate entity within Christendom, and by the end of the sixth century the "falling away" segment was established as the only recognized legal authority in Christianity. This is the so-called "Constantinian fall of the church."

The false doctrines embraced by the "falling away" church corrupted the apostolic faith in several areas: the belief that God is one was compromised by the doctrine of the trinity; justification by faith was replaced with justification by works; repentance was changed to penance; the name of Jesus Christ was deleted from the baptismal formula; receiving the Holy Ghost with the sign of speaking in tongues was discredited by teaching that the experience had ceased. These nonbiblical doctrines that corrupted, obscured, and contradicted apostolic doctrine became cardinal doctrines of the "falling away" church, which used the civil power of the state to force others to accept these doctrines or suffer, sometimes even to death.

In order to justify changing apostolic doctrines and adding others, "falling away" leaders proclaimed a doctrine of continuing revelations to the church by the Spirit. This was compounded by the doctrine of apostolic succession and the elevation of the office of the bishop. This enabled them to embrace "revelations" without the support of the Scriptures and to adopt interpretations that contradicted what the apostles taught.

It is not surprising, therefore, that efforts to leap over the false doctrines held by the "falling away" church in order to return to the "common salvation" taught and experienced by the apostolic church in the Book of Acts would be met with hostile and often violent opposition. Yet, in spite of persecution, people would read Jude's words, study the apostolic church in the Bible, and begin the return journey to apostolic doctrine and experience.

The Restoration Impulse

Until recent years apologists and critics have mostly focused on the most distinctive element in Pentecostalism, speaking in tongues. While the reception of the Spirit with the sign of tongues is the central doctrine in the emergence of Pentecostalism in 1901, the many doctrines, lifestyles, cultures, and church governments that emerged in the Pentecostal movement suggest that there are other lenses through which to view the movement.

One of these other lenses is the restoration impulse, the driving force to restore the apostolic church with the same salvation experience, doctrines, lifestyle, ministry, miracles, church government, and gifts of the Spirit. Edith Blumhofer, in *Restoring the Faith: The Assemblies of God, Pentecostalism, and American Culture*, suggests that the restoration impulse is the best method of identifying the Pentecostal movement.

The word restoration means "a putting or bringing back into a former, normal, or unimpaired state or condition; a representation or reconstruction of the original form or structure." Therefore, to restore is to "bring back to a former or normal condition" or "to bring back into being or use; to reestablish." The restoration impulse as defined by church historians is the impelling or driving

11

force to return to the salvation experience, teachings, practices, and ministry of the apostolic church.

We must acknowledge, however, that the restoration impulse is not the sole property of the Pentecostal movement, for it has been the inspiration that created movements since the early centuries after the apostolic age. It is also true that not all restorationist movements follow their initial goal to restore apostolic Christianity, for many follow faulty ideas, self-serving leaders, and nonbiblical doctrines. Sometimes a charismatic leader will claim to be a prophet or apostle with revelations and visions far from the teachings of the Bible. A few restorationist leaders attempt to build "Christian" communities, but often they pattern their communities not after the apostolic church in the New Testament but after perverted interpretations of Scriptures. Some "restorationist" communities resemble the Israelites under the Old Testament covenant and not the church in Acts. While some restorationist movements have come closer to the concepts of the apostolic church, at least at their beginnings, few have progressed beyond the doctrine and spirituality of wayward historic Christianity.

Throughout church history we find the restoration impulse in movements such as the Waldenses and Albigenses in France, the Lollards (followers of John Wycliffe) in England, the Hussites (followers of John Hus) in Moravia and Bohemia, the Protestant Reformation in Europe, the Wesleyan-Methodist-Holiness movement in North America, and Pentecostalism throughout the world, especially Oneness Pentecostalism.

Under severe persecution, the Waldenses and Albigenses survived in small groups, some uniting with the churches formed out of the Protestant Reformation. Although the magisterial reformers, Martin Luther, Ulrich Zwingli, and John Calvin were drawn toward restorationism, they used it only to reform the existing church and not to restore apostolic Christianity. Therefore they accepted doctrines formulated by the ecumenical councils of the early centuries and other teachings of the Roman Catholic Church. Yet, in their efforts to change practices, rituals, and rules of the church, they restored some apostolic teaching, particularly the doctrine of justification by faith.

We should note that the Radical Reformation as it developed alongside the Protestant Reformation was following the restoration impulse when they made a complete break with Catholicism, returned to believers' water baptism by immersion, embraced a lifestyle of holiness, and tried to create an apostolic church order and structure by separating the church from the state.

The restoration impulse emerged again in the Second Great Awakening in America (1790s-1840s). Thousands of people experienced a life-changing encounter with God in camp meetings that drew crowds of twenty to thirty thousand people. The force of this spiritual wave was felt across America, touching New England, reviving churches throughout the South, and reshaping the character of the Western frontier.

Some people in this revival discovered that the apostles administered water baptism in the name of Jesus Christ for the remission of sins, taught that the baptism of the Holy Ghost was a part of the plan of salvation, and did not mention the doctrine of the trinity. Yet they failed to restore these apostolic doctrines during the Awakening.

13

The Baptism of the Holy Ghost

The restoration impulse sparked by the Second Great Awakening became the guiding force in the Holiness movement, especially in the last half of the nineteenth century. By the time of the Holiness revival in 1857-58, some leaders had begun to identify the experience of sanctification as the baptism of the Holy Ghost. Later, others began teaching that the baptism of the Holy Ghost was an additional experience beyond sanctification. In his book, *The Theological Roots of Pentecostalism*, Donald Dayton traces the gradual doctrinal shift from sanctification as a second work of grace to the Pentecostal concept of the Holy Spirit baptism. He concludes, "The point of this is that by the mid-1890s almost every branch of the Holiness and 'higher life' movements of the nineteenth century, as well as revivalism of the period in general, was teaching a variation of some sort or another on the baptism of the Holy Ghost, though with some significant differences and nuances."

This shift toward biblical terminology and experience led Holiness leaders such as R. A. Torrey, president of Moody Bible Institute, to study the biblical sign of receiving the Holy Ghost. In his book, *The Baptism of the Holy Spirit*, first published in 1885, he wrote, "In my early study of the Baptism with the Holy Spirit, I noticed that in many instances those who were so baptized 'spoke with tongues,' and the question came often into my mind: if one is baptized with the Holy Spirit will he not speak with tongues? But I saw no one so speaking, and I often wondered, is there anyone today who actually is baptized with the Holy Spirit?"

Torrey's study of the baptism of the Holy Ghost led

14

him to the Bible sign of speaking in tongues at least fifteen years before Charles Fox Parham discovered it and made it the cornerstone of the Pentecostal revival. By 1901 the Holiness movement had led people to the doorstep and into the Pentecostal revival.

CHAPTER TWO

THE EARLY PENTECOSTAL REVIVAL

After Charles F. Parham's birth in 1873 in Muscatine, Iowa, the Parham family moved to Cheney, Kansas, a small town about twenty miles west of Wichita, Kansas. His mother died when he was twelve years old, and the next year his thoughts turned toward God and as a result he was converted in a Congregational church. At the age of fifteen, he taught Sunday school, and the next year he entered Southwestern Kansas College. However, his stay at the college was terminated when he left to become a Methodist minister.

As a young supply minister at the age of nineteen, Parham served as pastor of Methodist churches in towns southwest of Kansas City, but after two years he left the Methodists and evangelized in Holiness churches for the next four or five years. In 1898 he established a mission in Topeka, Kansas, and in the same year, he secured a large building and opened a faith healing home. People in need of healing could live in one of the fourteen rooms on the second floor while they were praying for divine healing.

Bethel Healing Home, Topeka, Kansas

On the ground floor, Parham conducted services, taught Bible studies to workers and ministers, and began publishing a magazine, *The Apostolic Faith.*

Two years later in October 1900, he turned the faith home over to two Holiness preachers and opened Bethel Bible College in a large building known as Stone's Folly. The school opened with about forty students.

When classes at the college recessed for the Christmas and New Year holidays, Parham assembled the students and asked them to study the Bible to find the indisputable sign of the baptism of the Holy Ghost. Although he later wrote that he himself had not searched the Scriptures for the sign, he said he felt sure that there was a definite sign given in the Scriptures. It appears that he had tentatively considered speaking in tongues as the sign, for he read Acts 2:1-4 to the students before he departed on a three-day preaching tour.

When Parham returned to the college, he called the students together and asked for their answer. To his sur-

Eramus Stone's Mansion, known as Stone's Folly, was the site for Charles Parham's Bethel Bible College

prise, every student had the same answer: The biblical sign of the baptism of the Holy Ghost is speaking in tongues.

On January 1, 1901, the first student, Agnes Ozman, received the Holy Ghost with the sign of speaking in tongues, and this event marked the beginning of what would be known as the Pentecostal revival and movement. On the evening of January 3, twelve other students received the Holy Ghost while praying in a room on the second floor of the college. Parham, who returned late that evening from preaching in a local church, heard the noise, entered the room, knelt, began praising God for this event, and asked God to give him this same blessing. In a few moments, he received the Holy Ghost with the

19

sign of speaking in tongues.

During the next few weeks and months, most of the students and many people from the city were filled with the Holy Ghost. Local newspapers carried stories about the happening, and newspapers as far away as Kansas City, Missouri, and St. Louis, Missouri, reported on the revival in Topeka.

During the summer months, Stone's Mansion was sold, forcing the college to move. Parham moved temporarily to another location in Topeka, but he soon moved to Kansas City, Missouri, where he opened a mission.

For the next two years, the small band of Pentecostals struggled. They opened a second mission in the nearby city of Lawrence, Kansas, and held meetings in several towns and communities. But growth was slow, finances were scarce, and persecution from churches made life difficult. Yet the group survived.

The Revival in Galena, Kansas

In the summer of 1903, an event in the small town of El Dorado Springs, Missouri, sparked a revival that soon transformed Pentecostalism into a movement. A woman who was converted in the mission in Lawrence opened a mission in Nevada, a small town in western Missouri. Parham and a few of his workers held a meeting in Nevada and then went to El Dorado Springs, which was only a few miles away. Parham knew that the mineral springs attracted many visitors each summer in search for healing. After Parham secured a house, the group held services near the steps going to the springs.

In August, Mary A. Arthur came to El Dorado Springs from her home in Galena, a mining town in southeastern

Kansas. For the past two summers she had visited the springs for treatment of several afflictions, the most distressful being an eye disease that caused a gradual loss of sight and a constant pain from light. She had undergone two operations on her eyes, but the deterioration of her vision and the pain continued, even though she wore two sets of sunglasses.

Mary Arthur

On August 17, Arthur was going to the springs when she heard Parham preaching on divine healing. Later that day she attended a service where Parham and his group were staying. At the end of the service, the workers prayed for her healing, and while she was returning to her room in the city, she discovered that her eyes were healed. Her sight was restored, and the pain was gone. When Arthur returned to her husband, family, and friends in Galena, everyone was amazed. She and her husband wrote Parham, asking him to hold a meeting in their home. A few weeks later Parham arrived in Galena, but the Arthurs' house was not large enough to hold the people who came. Parham was able to secure and erect a large tent on a nearby vacant lot. Soon crowds filled the tent, drawn by the many miracles of healing and people repenting of their sins and receiving the Holy Ghost with the sign of speaking in tongues.

When the weather began turning cold after Thanksgiving, Parham moved the meetings to the Grand Leader Building, a very large building that could accommodate about two thousand people. Yet the crowds grew so large

21

that people had to stand outside, and they did this in spite of the cold weather.

Newspapers as far away as St. Louis, Missouri, and Cincinnati, Ohio, reported on the revival in Galena. On January 1, 1904, the *St. Louis Globe Democrat* reported that more than five hundred people had been converted and a good number had already been baptized, but on this day another 250 people were immersed in the cold water of the river. Probably among those baptized in this service was Howard A. Goss, a young man who would become an important leader in the Pentecostal movement in general but particularly among Oneness Pentecostals.

On January 27, the *Cincinnati Enquirer* reported that eight hundred had been converted and at least one thousand people claimed to have been healed. Hundreds of people received the Holy Ghost during the meeting.

With the several hundred converts in the Galena revival, Parham built several churches in neighboring cities in Kansas, Missouri, and Oklahoma during 1904. This revival turned the Pentecostal revival into a movement. Parham named his group the Apostolic Faith movement and decided to establish headquarters for the movement in Baxter Springs, Kansas, a small town about eight miles west of Galena.

The Revival in Texas

The spread of Pentecostalism from Galena to Texas was the key to spreading Pentecostalism across North America and into nations around the world. During the fall of 1903, Mr. and Mrs. Walter Oyler, whose home was in Orchard, Texas, visited Joplin, Missouri. They attended Parham's meeting in the nearby city of Galena, and after

receiving the Holy Ghost, they stayed in Joplin the following year to help establish Pentecostal churches and
missions in the area. One of the workers they met was
Anna Hall, whom they invited to accompany them when
they returned home to Orchard.

The Oylers and Anna Hall arrived in Orchard in the
spring of 1905. This small rural town is located about
forty miles west of Houston. When Hall arrived, only a
few people in the town attended any church, but she held
services, and people showed interest in her message. She
then wrote Parham, urging him to come to Orchard as
soon as possible.

Parham's first service in Orchard was on Easter
Sunday in 1905. A crowd filled the meeting hall, and peo-
ple started seeking God. Many received the Holy Ghost.
In his report Parham wrote, "There were only five or six
Christians here, but in two weeks, there were only about
that many sinners."

Orchard had become the birthplace of the Pentecostal movement in Texas. For several years after 1905,
Parham held three-day meetings in Orchard at Easter as
a special time to commemorate that first meeting in Texas
and to bring the workers in Texas together for spiritual
renewal and fellowship.

Orchard was the door through which Pentecostalism came to Texas, but Houston became the center of
the movement for the state. Mrs. John C. Calhoun, who
attended a Holiness church in Brunner, a suburb of
Houston, visited Parham's meeting in Orchard. She told
her pastor, W. F. Carothers, about Parham's ministry and
the outpouring of the Holy Ghost. Carothers invited
Parham to preach at the Brunner church, which then was

converted to Pentecostalism.

On May 20, 1905, Parham returned to Baxter Springs to preach some camp meetings and special services, but in early July he returned to Texas with about twenty-five workers to evangelize in Houston and surrounding towns. Parham and his group conducted meetings, beginning on July 10 and lasting to the middle of August, in Bryan Hall in Houston, daily drawing large crowds. Scores of people received the Holy Ghost, and many notable healings occurred. This meeting with its large crowds, healings, and speaking in tongues introduced Pentecostalism to the city.

The group also held meetings in the surrounding towns of Richmond, Katy, Alvin, Angleton, Needleville, Crosby, and other nearby places. Again, many people received the Holy Ghost, and hundreds were brought into the movement.

Of particular importance among those who joined Parham was Lucy Farrow, a black pastor of a Holiness church in Houston. When Parham returned to Kansas in late August, Farrow was among those who accompanied him, and while she was in Kansas, she received the Holy Ghost.

In the middle of October, Parham returned to Houston with an additional fifteen workers. One of these workers was Howard Goss, whom Parham had baptized. At this time Goss had not yet received the baptism of the Holy Ghost.

The movement continued to grow so rapidly in and around Houston that in December Parham decided to establish a headquarters in Houston for the Apostolic Faith movement in Texas. In the same month, he opened a short-term Bible school in the city. His workers and local converts attended the school.

When Farrow left to go with Parham to Kansas, she turned her church over to a young black Holiness minister named William J. Seymour. Although schools in Texas were racially segregated at that time, Farrow persuaded Parham to allow Seymour to attend the Bible school in Houston. Seymour accepted Parham's teaching on the baptism of the Holy Ghost with the sign of speaking in tongues.

THE APOSTOLIC FAITH MOVEMENT

In early February 1906, Charles Parham's short-term Bible and training school in Houston ended, and he was ready to send out the large number of newly trained workers to establish missions in Houston and surrounding towns, as well as in other major cities in Texas and other states. This rapidly growing movement would now require some form of structure to keep the revival united. Although Parham was able to see the need for change and moved in that direction, the seeds of independence and distrust of organization that he himself had sown from the beginning of the movement would soon splinter and divide it in dozens of ways.

Restorationism in the Apostolic Faith Movement

Parham called his movement the Apostolic Faith, which was also the name of the paper he had begun publishing in 1898 after opening the faith healing home in Topeka, Kansas. The building he secured for this home was large enough to accommodate the many people who came to live there while they were praying for healing, and it provided a mission where they could worship and a place to publish *The Apostolic Faith*, a bimonthly paper. When he left the faith home and began Bethel Bible College, he continued to publish *The Apostolic Faith*, and it became the official paper of the movement.

In revival meetings, Parham sometimes advertised by a public parade in which workers carried signs bearing the name Apostolic Faith. Parham also used the word

Charles Parham with the Apostolic banner.

Pentecost to refer to the experience or outpouring of the Spirit, including the power and gifts of the Holy Ghost, but not as a designation of his followers.

The terms *Pentecost* and *Pentecostal* were used by Holiness groups to refer to the baptism of the Holy Ghost as the Pentecostal experience, but it did not include speaking in tongues as the sign. To them, the baptism of the Holy Ghost was the same experience as sanctification, with the sign of an inner witness. At least one Holiness group used *Pentecostal* in their name: the Pentecostal Church of the

Nazarene. However, after *Pentecostal* became the preferred designation of those who spoke in tongues, this organization dropped Pentecostal from its name in 1919 to avoid confusion with the Pentecostal movement.

Parham's use of Apostolic Faith reflects his search for the restoration of apostolic experience, doctrine, and practice, which eventually led him to the baptism of the Holy Ghost with the initial sign of speaking in tongues.

In his book, *A Voice Crying in the Wilderness*, published in 1902, he argued against trine baptism (to immerse three times), stating that the apostles used only one name, Jesus, in baptism and therefore immersed only one time. It is evident, then, that Parham's restoration impulse led him to discover water baptism in the name of Jesus Christ. During the revival in Galena, Kansas, Parham used the apostolic formula of baptizing in the name of Jesus Christ instead of the trinitarian formula when he baptized Howard Goss and others. However, when Parham later departed from much of his earlier restoration impulse, he returned to using the trinitarian formula.

In 1905 Parham defined the purpose of the Apostolic Faith movement to be "the restoring of primitive Christianity," sometimes referring to Jude 3 to support this purpose. For instance, in the *Galveston News* (Texas), the reporter wrote, "The Apostolic Successionists claim to be of no church and no creed; but to have for their sole purpose the 'restoration of the faith once delivered to the saints.'" In *A Voice Crying in the Wilderness*, Parham related the events of the outpouring of the Holy Ghost at Bethel Bible College, calling it "a marvelous restoration of apostolic power." He also adopted the Latter Rain motif of an end-time restoration of all spiritual gifts to the church.

Another interesting aspect of the Apostolic Faith movement was its insistence on not being called a church. They preferred to be viewed as the instrument that God was using to restore the apostolic faith and power to all denominations. It may have been for this reason that they referred to their meeting places as missions and not as churches. Of course, *mission* was an appropriate designation for storefronts and small rented buildings. Moreover, *missions* emphasized their evangelistic activities in distinction to established denominations. Further, *missions* served to contrast their informal, open, and spiritual emphasis in worship to the more formal, ritualistic, and established forms of worship in mainline churches.

The Growth of the
Apostolic Faith Movement

By the beginning of 1906, Apostolic Faith missions had been established not only in Kansas, Missouri, and Oklahoma but also in several places in Texas: Alvin, Galveston, Orchard, Houston, Brunner, and Wallis. Howard Goss assisted in establishing missions in Alvin, Galveston, and Wallis. He said that the mission in Alvin became a revival center in its area.

By the summer of 1906, the Apostolic Faith movement had grown from about 300 members to about 13,000 followers in an area from Texas to Kansas. (The number of 13,000 is reported in the September 1906 issue of *The Apostolic Faith* published by the Azusa Street Mission in Los Angeles.) But the movement's growth would soon accelerate even faster because the revival at the Azusa Street Mission in Los Angeles would soon sweep across North America and around the world.

Moreover, Parham's ministry sparked a tremendous revival in Zion City, Illinois, adding 2,000 followers in this city and spreading the movement into Canada and into the Northeastern states, including New York City.

This was a phenomenal period of growth. By the summer of 1908, the number of members in the Apostolic Faith movement had grown to an estimated membership of 25,000. The continued revival that began at the Azusa Street Mission in Los Angeles along with the growth in Texas and the Midwest soon added scores of thousands to the movement in North America. By 1910, several Holiness organizations and hundreds of other churches were converted to the Pentecostal experience. Although the Pentecostal movement was dismissed by most mainline churches as being of little importance, it was poised to become the third force in Christendom.

From Bible School to . . .

When the Bible and training school in Houston ended in early February 1906, Parham counseled with each student about the place he was to take the message of the Apostolic Faith movement. Usually, Parham assigned two students to work together in establishing a mission in a town.

He gave Howard Goss and another student a silver dollar each and sent them south toward Mexico, not naming any town in which they should start a mission. The two workers stopped briefly in Alvin, where they were given some more money by believers, and then on February 27, 1906, they began meetings in the courthouse auditorium in Angleton. They were given permission to hold a few meetings without rent, but they soon secured an abandoned saloon in which to hold meetings regularly.

Success, however, did not come quickly or easily. They attracted about a dozen people to come inside the building. Sometimes a few others stood outside the door but would not come in. This lasted for the next several weeks. Since they believed that God would provide all their needs for them, they refused—and may have been forbidden—to ask for financial help or to even hint to the people of their financial needs. Consequently, they often went without food—once for three days. The lack of food paralleled the meetings, for the first several weeks they saw no results. But when the revival broke, they received financial support to provide food. Goss wrote, "I preached every night for seven weeks before a break came. But when God did begin to do things, the bottom of heaven seemed to fall out." He reported that "scores were saved, healed, and filled with the Spirit"—and they at last had enough food.

The Holy Ghost Train Ride

While Howard Goss was helping to establish a mission in Angleton, Texas, he received an announcement from Parham that all workers in Texas were to meet in Orchard, Texas, on April 13-15, 1906, for a convention. The date was over the Easter holiday, and it marked the first anniversary of the Apostolic Faith movement in Texas. Several hundred people attended this convention. The small town of Orchard offered Parham and his workers a place of rest from the struggle of mission work. For Goss, this convention also offered an opportunity for him to receive the Holy Ghost.

From the first day of the convention, Goss earnestly prayed for God to fill him with the Spirit, but each serv-

Howard and Millicent Goss

ice and day ended in disappointment. After the service on the last night, he continued to pray until dawn.

Special arrangements had been made with the railroad to add extra cars for the many workers returning to Houston and other areas. In the morning the workers all gathered at the station to board the train, but it was late. Waiting, the workers began singing, worshiping, and praying. Parham then preached for a while, and the Spirit began falling upon them.

When the train came, the Holy Ghost was still blessing them, and when they boarded, Parham decided to go with them at least as far as the first stop. On the train, the Spirit continued to move among them, and Goss and other workers needing the Spirit opened their hearts to receive the Spirit. He explained it this way: "When another great bolt of God's lightning struck me, thereby loosening me still further, I began to speak in strange tongues, as the Spirit actually did the speaking." Goss later learned that as the train hastened its way toward their cities, twelve people had received the baptism of the

Apostolic Faith gathering in September 1906 at Brunner Tabernacle. Charles Parham is standing to the left front of the right upright beam. Howard Goss is standing on the extreme right of the first row.

Holy Ghost in his coach and five in another coach, for a total of seventeen. As Goss put it, "What a train ride!"

Brunner Tabernacle and Camp Meeting

In the summer of 1906, Parham and W. F. Carothers gathered the workers for a camp meeting in Brunner, a suburb of Houston. They constructed a large wooden tabernacle for a camp meeting, the first tabernacle built by the Apostolic Faith movement. Howard Goss, one of the workers on the tabernacle, was in for several good things during the camp meeting, which began on August 3 and was to end three weeks later. Heavy rains, however, made it impossible to conduct the baptism service planned for the last day, so the meeting was extended one day to baptize the forty-four new converts. They reported that at least 2,000 people attended the baptism service in the White Oak bayou. Brunner Tabernacle would become the place of an annual camp meeting for many years.

At this meeting, Parham took the first steps to organize the Apostolic Faith movement. Previously, the work had been loosely held together by his leadership and charisma, but the tremendous growth needed a structure to keep the movement united and focused. Parham took the title of projector of the Apostolic Faith movement, and he appointed Carothers to be the general field director and Goss to be the director of the work in Texas. He ordained and issued ministerial credentials to the workers. Goss's credentials show that he was ordained as an elder and minister of the Apostolic Faith movement. Both Carothers, as field director, and Parham, as projector, signed Goss's credentials. One other good thing happened to Goss during this camp meeting: He and Millicent McClendon became engaged to be married.

CHAPTER FOUR

THE AZUSA STREET REVIVAL

William Joseph Seymour, a black Holiness preacher living in Houston, attended Parham's Bible and training school in Houston, and he became the most widely known early Pentecostal. Seymour, born in Centerville, Louisiana, on May 2, 1870, was reared in the Baptist church. In 1895, he moved to Indianapolis, Indiana, where he joined a local congregation of the Methodist Episcopal Church. While in Indianapolis, he became ill with smallpox, which left him blind in his left eye. In 1900 he moved to Cincinnati, Ohio, where he became interested in the Holiness doctrine of entire sanctification. After accepting this teaching, he was licensed and ordained to be a minister in a Holiness group known as the Evening Light Saints.

In 1903 Seymour moved to Houston and attended a Holiness church pastored by Lucy F. Farrow. In 1905 Farrow, who had been born into slavery in Norfolk, Virginia, met Charles Parham in Houston, and she became convinced of his message of the baptism of the Holy Ghost. When Parham returned to Kansas in the summer of

1905 to preach camp meetings and to recruit more work-
ers for Houston, Farrow left her church in the care of
Seymour, and she and others went with Parham to
Kansas. While in Kansas, she received the baptism of the
Holy Ghost.

When Parham opened the Bible and training school
in Houston, Farrow was hired to be the cook, and she
became the link to get Seymour into the school. Although
schools in Texas were segregated at that time, she encouraged Parham to allow Seymour to enroll and attend classes.
As a good student, Seymour quickly became grounded in
the Apostolic Faith doctrine.

Sometime during 1905, Neely Terry, a young woman
from a black Holiness mission in Los Angeles, visited
Houston and met Seymour at the Holiness church. She
told Seymour that the Holiness mission she attended on
Santa Fe Avenue in Los Angeles was looking for a pastor
and asked if he would be interested in coming to
California to consider pastoring the mission. She
informed him that Julia W. Hutchins was temporarily fill-
ing in as pastor.

When Neely Terry returned to Los Angeles, she told
the members of the mission about Seymour. Taking her
recommendation, the congregation wrote to Seymour,
asking him to move to Los Angeles and to assume the
pastorate of their mission.

When Seymour told Parham about the offer in Los
Angeles, Parham did not favor it. First of all, Seymour had
not received the Holy Ghost. Second, Parham felt that he
should stay in Houston and work among the large black
population in the city. However, when Parham saw that
Seymour had decided to go to Los Angeles, he raised

money for his train fare and other travel expenses.

Seymour arrived in Los Angeles on February 22, 1906. The next Sunday morning he preached at the mission, using Acts 2:1-4 as his text. The focus of his message was that speaking in tongues was the sign of the gift of the Holy Ghost, a doctrine that did not meet with the approval of Julia Hutchins. When Seymour returned for the evening service, he found the mission locked in order to keep him out.

Although the Edward S. Lee family, who attended the Holiness mission, did not necessarily agree with Seymour's Apostolic Faith message, they felt they should invite him to stay awhile with them, at least until he could make arrangements to return to Houston. He accepted, and in their home he began prayer services. For the next week or two, Seymour held prayer services in the Lee home and gradually won their trust and belief in the baptism of the Holy Ghost. When Seymour accepted the invitation of the Richard Asberry family to move the prayer services to their home at 214 Bonnie Brae Street, he continued to live in the Lee home.

Among those who visited the prayer meetings in the Lee home was Frank Bartleman, where he met Seymour. Later, on March 26, Bartleman visited the prayer service at the Asberry home on Bonnie Brae Street. This was about two weeks before the first outpouring of the Holy Ghost.

The Outpouring of the Spirit

Toward the end of March or the first of April, Lucy Farrow arrived in Los Angeles to help Seymour. She had traveled from Houston with J. A. Warren, another member of the Apostolic Faith movement. On April 9, 1906, before Seymour left the Lee home to go to the Asberry home, Edward Lee asked Seymour to lay hands on him and pray that he would receive the Holy Ghost. Farrow also was involved in the prayer with the laying on of hands. Within moments Lee began speaking in tongues.

When Seymour told the small group praying in the Asberry home about Lee receiving the Holy Ghost, the Spirit fell on several of the women, including Jennie Evans Moore. Three days later, Seymour himself received the Holy Ghost. On the following Sunday morning, April 15, Jennie Moore attended the Easter service at her church, the New Testament Church, a congregation that had split from the large First Baptist Church in their search for a revival of Pentecostal power. At the end of the morning service, Moore spoke in tongues, creating a stir among the people.

When it became known to the congregation that the Holy Ghost had fallen upon the prayer group on Bonnie Brae Street, scores of them decided to attend the prayer service that evening. Bartleman was at the New Testament Church service and heard Moore speak in tongues, and he was among the crowd of people who came to the Asberry home that evening. The house was small, so the people filled the yard and street in front of the house, and the meeting was therefore held outside.

The Azusa Street Mission

By Tuesday, April 17, Seymour had secured an old frame abandoned two-story building on Azusa Street in the center of the city. The building had been used at various times as a Methodist church, a stable, and a warehouse. A reporter for the *Los Angeles Times* attended the

The Azusa Street Mission

first service on this date and referred to the building as a "tumble-down shack."

On April 18, the terrible earthquake hit San Francisco. Bartleman reported that on Thursday, April 19, occasional tremors would still shake buildings even in Los Angeles. On that evening he made his first visit to the Azusa Street meeting. He wrote, "We finally reached 'Azusa' and found about a dozen saints there, some white, some colored. Brother Seymour was there, in charge." He wrote that the building "had become a receptacle for old lumber, plaster, etc. They had cleared space enough in the surrounding dirt and debris to lay some planks on top of empty nail kegs, with seats enough for possibly thirty people." He remarked, "The 'Ark of God' moved off slowly, but surely at 'Azusa.'"

The revival started slowly, but by the first of August

it had exploded into overflowing crowds day and night. There were three services conducted each day, but Bartleman stated that the building was never closed. At times, crowds of 300-350 people pushed their way into the forty-by-sixty-foot building. And people came from everywhere. Bartleman wrote, "All classes began to flock to the meetings." He remarked, "It seemed that everyone had to go to 'Azusa.'" Many people attended out of curiosity, but most came with a hunger for God.

During three years of continuous revival at the Azusa Street Mission, thousands of people received the Holy Ghost. Many of them were pastors, missionaries, evangelists, and church leaders, and these and hundreds of others took the Pentecostal message across the United States, Mexico, Canada, South America, and overseas to Africa, Asia, and Europe. For three years, Azusa became the center of the Pentecostal revival, spreading the Pentecostal experience to regions around the globe.

The Azusa Street Revival

We should keep in mind the difference between the revival experienced in the mission located in a barn-like building on Azusa Street in Los Angeles and the revival it ignited in cities, states, and nations. The glorious revival at the Azusa Street Mission was to fade and end in three years, but the revival it began beyond its walls still burns brilliantly across the landscape of the world.

The outpouring of the Holy Ghost in Los Angeles happened because several favorable conditions harmonized. First, Parham's doctrinal formulation of speaking in tongues as the sign of the baptism of the Holy Ghost was crucial in igniting the revival in Topeka in 1901, but it was also vital in sparking the revival in Los Angeles. Since Seymour had accepted Parham's doctrine while attending the Bible school in Houston, he carried and used this key in Los Angeles.

Second, people in Los Angeles were seeking a spiritual renewal before Seymour arrived in the city on February 22, 1906. In 1905 Dr. Joseph Smale, pastor of the First Baptist Church in Los Angeles, traveled to Wales to investigate the Welsh Revival under Evan Roberts. After he returned, he and Elmer K. Fisher, pastor of the First Baptist Church in Glendale, California, began holding congregational prayer meetings to seek for an outpouring of the Holy Ghost.

When Smale was forced to leave the pastorate of the Baptist church, he organized the New Testament Church with people who followed him. Although at the time he knew nothing about the sign of speaking in tongues, he preached and prayed for an outpouring of the Spirit. Fisher, Frank Bartleman, and others often attended prayer services at the New Testament Church, and in one of the services, Fisher received the Holy Ghost with the sign of speaking in tongues.

Jennie Moore, who received the Holy Ghost on April 9, 1906, during Seymour's prayer meeting in the home of Richard and Ruth Asberry on Bonnie Brae Street, was a member of the New Testament Church. The next Sunday, April 15, she testified of receiving the Holy Ghost in the morning service, causing many of the congregation to gather at the Asberry home that evening.

Smale himself sought the baptism of the Spirit with the sign of tongues but never experienced it. At length he rejected the doctrine of tongues and called the revival at the Azusa Street Mission fanaticism. As a result, most of those who had received the Spirit left his congregation to open a Pentecostal mission under the leadership of Fisher on South Spring Street, only a few blocks from the Azusa Street Mission. This mission, known as the Upper Room Mission, would play an important role in the movement. Like other leaders of Pentecostal missions in Los Angeles, Fisher accepted the prominent role of the Azusa Street Mission, but he promoted some distinctions from Azusa in forms of worship.

Frank Bartleman, having moved to Los Angeles in December1904, became a part of the early prayer groups seeking the outpouring of the Spirit in Los Angeles. He attended the New Testament Church and often ministered in the small Holiness missions in the city. In March and April of 1906 he attended some of the prayer meetings held by Seymour in the Lee home and later in the Asberry home. He also wrote and distributed evangelistic tracts, did personal evangelism in the city, and corresponded with Evan Roberts.

Bartleman created a climate for an outpouring of the Holy Ghost through the articles he submitted to Holiness publications. During 1905 many of his articles appeared in Holiness papers in the Midwest and South, especially the *Way of Faith* in Columbia, South Carolina; *God's Revivalist* in Cincinnati, Ohio; and *Christian Harvester*. After the outpouring of the Spirit in Los Angeles, he continued to write articles for these same papers, reporting on the revival at the Azusa Street Mission. His articles captured the interest of Holiness believers, preparing them to become a part of the Pentecostal movement.

Third, a spiritual spark was needed to ignite the

revival, and this spark came with Lucy Farrow, who had come from Houston a short time before April 9, 1906. It was Farrow who laid hands on Edward Lee when he was baptized with the Holy Ghost. Lee was the first person in Seymour's meetings to receive the Holy Ghost, and when Lee began speaking in tongues in the home on Bonnie Brae Street, six others received the Holy Ghost. Three days later, on April 12, Seymour received the Holy Ghost.

The Growing Revival in Los Angeles

The small group of Pentecostals in the Azusa Street Mission grew slowly at first, but soon the building started to become full. By August 1906 the revival had spread into several Holiness congregations in Los Angeles and its suburbs. Several local ministers, including A. G. Garr, Glenn Cook, Thomas Hezmalhalch, A. H. Post, Florence Crawford, Frank Bartleman, Elmer K. Fisher, and William Pendleton received the Holy Ghost, most of them at the Azusa Street Mission. People from the more spiritual churches in Los Angeles began pouring into the Azusa Street Mission. Bartleman wrote that "Holiness meetings, tents, and missions began to close up for lack of attendance. Their people were at 'Azusa.' Brother and Sister Garr closed the 'Burning Bush' hall, came to 'Azusa,' received the 'baptism,' and were on their way to India to spread the fire."

When William Pendleton and his Holiness congregation became Pentecostal, they lost their church building. Bartleman invited Pendleton to move his congregation to the mission he had started in a church building at Eighth Street and Maple Avenue, and this mission became an important center of revival.

In an article dated August 1, 1906, "Pentecost has come to Los Angeles," in the *Way of Faith*, a Holiness paper edited by J. M. Pike, Bartleman reported that, in spite of opposition from churches and the struggle against fanaticism in the services, the meetings at the Azusa Street Mission "are crowded out." He wrote that "demons are being cast out, the sick healed, many blessedly saved, restored, and baptized with the Holy Ghost and power." He also predicted that "the revival will be a world-wide one, without doubt."

Working at the Azusa Street Mission

About a dozen people left their employment to become full-time workers at the Azusa Street Mission. These included Glenn Cook (a former Holiness minister), Clara E. Lum (a former white servant in the home of Parham), Florence Crawford, Hiram Smith (a former Methodist pastor), Jennie Moore, Ivey Campbell, and R. J. Scott (a minister from Canada). A room in the mission served as the business office, a large room upstairs was used as a place where people could tarry for the baptism of the Holy Ghost, and other upstairs rooms served as work areas and living quarters. A cottage behind the mission was also used for living quarters.

The workers ministered in the services, evangelized in Los Angeles and other cities, prayed with and assisted people at the altar, and did other needed tasks. No one was paid a salary; they depended upon the offerings that came into the collection box that hung on the wall in the auditorium. Glenn Cook, whose ministry later played an important role in spreading the Oneness message, served as the business manager for the mission, and he also worked on

46

William Seymour is sitting on the left of the front row.

The Apostolic Faith paper published at the mission.

Seymour, described as a humble servant of God, was the recognized leader of the mission. Bartleman acknowledged Seymour's leadership role but expressed the feeling of equality among the workers: "Brother Seymour was recognized as the nominal leader. But we had no pope or hierarchy. We were 'brethren.' We had no human programme. The Lord Himself was leading. We had no priest class, nor priest craft. These things have come in later, with the apostatizing of the movement. We did not even have a platform or pulpit in the beginning. We were on a level."

Bartleman attributed part of the success of the Azusa

Street revival to the seasoned workers: "One reason for the depth of the work at 'Azusa' was the fact that the workers were not novices. They were largely called and prepared for years, from the Holiness ranks, and from the mission field. . . . They were largely seasoned veterans."

Reaching California and Beyond

By the end of 1906, evangelists and workers traveling from the Azusa Street Mission had opened missions in most of the major cities in California, established a large work in Portland, Oregon, reached into Washington, and converted at least one congregation in Canada to Pentecostalism.

The West Coast, however, was only the springboard toward worldwide revival. In November and December, ministers from the Azusa Street Mission began taking the Pentecostal message east, especially to the Midwest: Glenn Cook took the message to Oklahoma, Missouri, Indiana, and Tennessee; Ivey Campbell went to Ohio; and Tom Hezmalhalch opened missions in Colorado. The message they carried sparked revivals in churches and cities, adding thousands to the mushrooming Pentecostal movement.

Reading and hearing about the revival at the Azusa Street Mission, foreign missionaries came to Azusa to receive the Holy Ghost. They then returned to their missionary fields to spread the revival abroad. Moreover, several individuals and families who had not been missionaries felt called to the mission field, and they departed from Los Angeles to go to nations in Africa, Europe, Asia, South America, and the Middle East. During the next several years, reports from Pentecostal missionaries revealed the tremendous revivals ignited in these nations.

The Apostolic Faith **Paper**

One effective tool that helped in making the Azusa Street revival a worldwide revival was *The Apostolic Faith* paper published by the workers at the mission. In September 1906, they published the first issue, calling it the same name as Parham's paper, which he had begun publishing in 1898. They also adopted Parham's policy of publishing and distributing the paper by faith without subscription, solely depending upon God to prompt people to send offerings to pay the expenses. The mission continued to publish the paper through thirteen issues over a period of almost two years. The last issue was in May 1908.

The Apostolic Faith had a wide circulation as well as a wide influence on the revival. The first issue was for 5,000 copies. The demand then caused them to print and distribute 10,000 copies for the second issue, 20,000 for the third, 30,000 for the fourth. Later distribution reached 40,000 copies. This paper often inspired readers to begin praying immediately for the baptism of the Holy Ghost. It prepared and prompted thousands of people in North America and in nations around the world to believe God for an outpouring of the Holy Ghost in their areas.

The reports in *The Apostolic Faith* reveal some of the impact of the revival as it exploded in one place after another. Each issue pulsates with healings, baptisms of the Holy Ghost, miracles, and excited faith in action. It is little wonder that reading this paper drew the attention of multitudes, causing them to wonder and to hunger for the Pentecostal outpouring upon themselves.

The Apostolic Faith stirred missionaries, pastors, and revival-hungry people everywhere. Upon reading the reports, ministers and missionaries longed to be in the services at the humble building that housed the Azusa Street Mission. (We should note that the parents of David F. Gray and Olive [Gray] Haney, who were serving as missionaries in Asia, learned about the revival in Los Angeles, and when they were able to return to the United States, they visited the Azusa Street Mission and later received the Holy Ghost.)

Bartleman's reports and articles in Holiness publications also helped to create a climate for the Pentecostal outpouring among Holiness groups. He wrote more than 550 articles promoting Pentecostal revival, which were published in Holiness papers both before and after the revival began in Los Angeles. His articles caused people to seek the Pentecostal experience and drew many ministers and others to the Azusa Street Mission to investigate and to receive the Holy Ghost.

CHAPTER FIVE

THE ZION REVIVAL

During the last months of 1906, several events served as a springboard for the Pentecostal movement to mushroom into a worldwide movement. One of these events was Parham's revival in Zion, Illinois, for it brought into the Pentecostal movement not only about two thousand converts but also many experienced ministers and leaders among them. It also opened the door to reach Zion gatherings in many other cities in North America and even in several foreign nations, and many of these gatherings were converted to Pentecostalism and some became centers of Pentecostal revival and evangelism.

Revival in Zion

A remarkable revival that is not well known today even among Pentecostals made the unique city of Zion, Illinois, the second most significant center, after Azusa, in the spreading of the Pentecostal message throughout the world.

To understand why Zion is important, we will briefly trace the life and ministry of John Alexander Dowie, who founded Zion, one of the unique cities in the United States, built in 1900 to 1903 to be a city of peace and godliness.

John Alexander Dowie

Few people today would recognize the name of John Alexander Dowie or know of the remarkable story of his ministry, but at the beginning of this century, he was widely known in North America, England, Scotland, Australia, and other nations. Born on May 27, 1847, in Edinburgh, Scotland, Dowie lived his childhood in poverty, was frequently absent from classes at school, and was often sick. But he was a precocious child, reading any book he could obtain—it is said that he read the Bible through at age six—and at an early age, he developed a hatred of sin because he saw the suffering that evil brought to people.

When he was thirteen years of age, his family immigrated to Australia, but by working he was able to save enough funds to return to Scotland, where he entered Edinburgh University. After three years at the university, he returned to Australia and soon afterward decided to enter the ministry. In April 1872 he accepted the pastorate of a Congregational church in Alma but resigned in December. However, during the short months at Alma, a terrible plague swept across that part of Australia, taking the lives of thousands. In three weeks he officiated at forty funerals, and thirty other members were suffering from the plague. It was during this crisis that he came to believe in and to practice divine healing with astonishing success. When he started believing God for healing, not another person in his congregation died from the plague.

Dowie quickly moved through two more Congregational pastorates—at Manly Beach in 1874 and at Newton, a suburb of Sydney, in 1875 to 1877. While he was still at Newton, he married his cousin Jeanie in May 1876, although her father was not in favor of the marriage. He had been reluctant to give his consent since it would be a marriage between relatives and because of the restless behavior of Dowie. In the fall of 1877, the couple had their first child, a son, John Alexander Gladstone, and later they had a daughter, Esther.

In the spring of 1878, Dowie withdrew from the Congregational organization and opened an independent church in Sydney, but the venture ended in failure in 1882. He began planning to build a tabernacle in Melbourne, and in February 1883, he organized the Free Christian Church. In 1884 the tabernacle was completed, and when miracles of healing began to happen, the tabernacle became full and then overflowed. Soon Dowie was preaching not only in the tabernacle but also in open-air meetings in the streets and in parks. Once he

Alexander Dowie

preached to an audience of about 20,000 people. In the midst of this success, Dowie founded The International Divine Healing Association, which soon opened branches in various areas of Australia and New Zealand.

In late 1887 he and his family began a trip to England by way of America, stopping first in New Zealand to strengthen the branch works in that nation before sailing to San Francisco. When Dowie, his family, and several of his followers arrived in San Francisco on June 7, 1888, newspaper reporters met him to get a story. Dowie refused to give any interviews, but he allowed his followers to give their testimonies of healing. The news that Dowie was in San Francisco brought people of all classes to his hotel to seek his prayers for their healing. Believing that their faith was not in God, he refused to pray for any of them until one day he noticed a poor older woman with a crutch. After talking with her and being assured of her faith, he offered a short prayer for her healing. Immediately she was healed and left the crutch with him.

After several other notable miracles of healing occurred in San Francisco, Dowie held a series of healing campaigns along the West Coast, attracting large crowds, and many people were healed and converted. In 1889 he held campaigns in the Northwest and then traveled through several states and cities to the East. In the summer of 1890, he made his home in Evanston, Illinois, a suburb of Chicago, from which he launched campaigns in cities of the Midwest.

On August 7, 1890, during Dowie's address at a divine healing convention in Chicago, a woman in the audience asked Dowie if he would pray for Jennie Paddock, who was lying at her home, suffering from a fibroid tumor. Since mortification had set in, the doctors had abandoned the case as hopeless. Dowie prayed, the lady was healed, and the newspapers considered the healing so remarkable that a complete account of the healing appeared in several Chicago newspapers.

In 1893 Dowie moved into Chicago and built a small

wooden tabernacle not far from the gate to the World's Fair held in Chicago that year. The first service was held on May 7, 1893; however, only a few people came in for a visit, and fewer still attended the services. The next spring people began attending meetings at the tabernacle, and when news of healings spread, people soon filled the tabernacle at each service. At this time Dowie began publishing a weekly magazine, *Leaves of Healing*, to spread the testimonies of healing to the world, and soon people began coming from near and far. At this time his following in Chicago numbered a few thousand people.

In late 1894, Dowie began operating healing homes at which the sick could stay while praying for healing, but this move was seized by those who opposed Dowie as an opportunity to run him out of Chicago. They pressured the city council to pass a "hospital ordinance" to force Dowie to close the homes and perhaps to leave the city. When Dowie refused to comply, they persuaded the State Board of Health to charge him with practicing medicine without a license. During the next year, Dowie was arrested no less than one hundred times for violating the "hospital ordinance"; however, Dowie fought the ordinance in court and eventually won when the Cook County Superior Court declared the ordinance unconstitutional.

The publicity from his persecution merely served to attract more people, and consequently his movement experienced accelerated growth into several thousands. In the fall of 1895, Dowie leased one of the largest auditoriums in the city for six months and spoke each Sunday from October 27, 1895, to April 21, 1896. Four thousand attended the first service, but on subsequent Sundays, the crowds overflowed the seating capacity of six thousand.

Among his followers were many professional and business people, including ministers, teachers, lawyers, architects, and doctors, as well as people with talents and skills and wealth. Among the hundreds of people who testified of outstanding healings were some who were notable, such as Amanda Hicks, a first cousin of Abraham Lincoln; Jean Harrison, a niece of President Harrison; a Mrs. Lucas, wife of Colonel W. V. Lucas, a former congressman from South Dakota; and Sadie Cody, a niece of Buffalo Bill. The report of these healings made Dowie known throughout North America.

On February 5, 1896, Dowie organized the Christian Catholic Church, a step that he had carefully planned. Dowie assumed the title of general overseer. Two years later, on September 18, 1898, Dowie organized the Zion Seventies, who were commissioned to evangelize every home in Chicago, to distribute literature, and to invite people to meetings.

The Zion Seventies soon grew to 3,000 members, and due to their work, thousands of people came to Zion services. Moreover, many branch Zion tabernacles were started in Chicago and in many other cities in North America, such as Cincinnati, Cleveland, New York City, Boston, St. Louis, Kansas City, Houston, and San Antonio. Furthermore, branches were opened in Canada, Australia, South Africa, England, Scotland, Germany, and other countries in Europe.

The Building of Zion

During the years of 1898 and 1899, Dowie clandestinely worked on another project: the building of Zion, a city where people could live free from a wicked and corrupting society. With special agents sworn to secrecy, Dowie embarked on the purchase of 6,500 acres of farmland located forty miles north of Chicago on Lake Michigan. The land was purchased and surveyed, the city was plotted, plans for houses and a school were drawn up, and locations for businesses were established. Dowie also commissioned a large painting of the proposed city.

On the first day of 1900, Dowie unveiled his plan to the Zion congregation and received their enthusiastic approval. On July 14, 1900, Zion members went to the proposed site of Zion City, and Dowie turned the first sod.

On July 15, 1901, the first area was opened for families to lease lots on which to build their homes. The Elijah Hospice, one of the largest frame buildings in America, was finished and made ready for its guests to stay as they built their homes. The building of houses began almost immediately, and by the summer of 1902, many of them were finished. Factories were operating, businesses were open, and the place began to look like a city. Dowie predicted that in five years the city would have a population of 50,000 and eventually 200,000, but these projections were not to be. By 1906, the city had reached a population of only about 10,000. Today the population is about 23,000.

Zion City was only the first phase in Dowie's plan, merely a stepping-stone to the building of other Zion cities all over the world. The largest city would be a rebuilt Jerusalem. All this was in preparation for the return of Christ to set up His millennial kingdom on earth. Christ would then rule from this rebuilt Jerusalem, and His people would rule under Him from Zion cities.

Elijah the Prophet

In June 1901, the month when people started building their homes in Zion, Dowie made a startling declaration: He identified himself as Elijah the Restorer, the Prophet foretold by Moses in Deuteronomy 18:18-19, and the Messenger of the Covenant in fulfillment of Malachi 3:1-3. This troubled some of his followers, for they noted that the two Bible passages referred to none other than Jesus Christ. When Dowie organized the Restoration Host, he required the members to vow that they acknowledged him to be the one who was to fulfill these prophecies.

The First Apostle

Late in the summer of 1904, less than three months after he finished an around-the-world tour, Dowie made another declaration, this time proclaiming that he was not only Elijah but also the First Apostle of Jesus Christ in the Christian Catholic Church. When he finished making this declaration in Shiloh Tabernacle in Zion City, he asked the congregation, "Do you accept me?" Although the people went along with his declaration, many, if not most of them, had serious doubts about what was happening to their general overseer.

The Fall of Dowie

The financial collapse of Zion became a certainty in early 1905 when Dowie refused to listen when his over-seers warned him that financial problems were pushing the city toward bankruptcy. Dowie, who considered the money in the banks to be his, had taken hundreds of thousands of dollars from the bank accounts for a Restoration Host crusade in New York City, his tour around the world, and personal expenses. The factories were therefore left with little or no cash to purchase raw materials for operations. People's savings were depleted and creditors were being paid late, if at all. Yet Dowie refused to believe that the city was in any serious trouble.

Then on September 24, 1905, Dowie suffered a stroke as he was finishing a sermon in Shiloh Tabernacle. The stroke left his body partially paralyzed on his right side. Although hope was expressed that he would have a full recovery, it never happened. While he did improve some, he was never the same again.

When Dowie went south to rest in the warm climate and to recover, he cabled Wilbur Glenn Voliva, his trusted overseer of the Zion work in Australia, requesting him to come to Zion and take over the affairs until he returned. Dowie gave Voliva full power of authority to act as general overseer.

After Voliva arrived in Zion City on February 12, 1906, he examined the financial records and books, recognized the disaster confronting the city, and with the overseers deposed Dowie from his position of general overseer. At a town meeting held on April 1, 1906, Voliva and the overseers asked the people to approve their action, which they did. Voliva then sent a message to Dowie suspending him from his position of general overseer.

Dowie returned to fight, but he had already lost the support of the people. The city faced a debt of six million dollars. In August 1906 a civil court judge, Kenesaw Landis, listened to both Dowie's and Voliva's sides and then placed the city into the hands of a receiver, changed the government to be democratic, and ordered an election to determine who would be the general overseer of the church. Dowie, knowing that he could not win, did not run, and Voliva was elected.

Although Dowie tried to gather a following, his health continued to decline, and on March 9, 1907, he died after a prolonged and painful sickness.

Events Leading to the
Pentecostal Revival in Zion

Charles Parham already knew about Dowie's Zion movement, for in the spring of 1900 he had visited Dowie's work in Chicago on his trip to the East to learn what other restorationist movements were doing. Parham may have also heard news about the city of Zion from a woman, Mrs. Waldron, who had received the Holy Ghost in 1902 while attending Parham's mission in Lawrence, Kansas. Waldron moved to Zion in 1904 and began prayer meetings in her home. Soon a Mrs. Hall received the baptism of the Holy Ghost, creating a stir in the city. Waldron and Hall lost their jobs, and they were forced to leave Zion to find employment. When another woman, Louise Albach, accepted the Pentecostal message, Dowie forced her to resign her school position. But in spite of Dowie's opposition, he could only postpone, and not stop, the coming Pentecostal revival in Zion.

Daniel Charles Owen Opperman

In 1900 D. C. O. Opperman joined the Zion movement in Chicago, and in 1902 Dowie ordained him into the ministry. Opperman served as a principal in the school system in Zion and as a teacher in Zion College. In the fall of 1905, he became ill with tuberculosis and took leave of his duties. In an effort to recover his health in a warm climate, he went to Texas, where he visited with Lemuel C. Hall, the leader of the Zion branch in San Antonio. Opperman went to Houston, and while he was there, God spoke to him, telling him to preach on the streets of the city. When he obeyed, he received his healing.

Opperman returned to Zion to finish the school term, but the next year he resigned his position and returned to Houston. In March 1906, he met Parham in Houston, and Parham convinced him that the Pentecostal message of the baptism of the Holy Ghost with the sign of speaking in tongues was biblical.

Parham had recently finished the Bible school in Houston and had sent the workers to various cities to evangelize and to establish churches. In April he would conduct the annual convention in Orchard for the workers before he returned to Kansas.

Opperman remained in Texas with Parham and accompanied him to Galena to attend an Apostolic Faith convention there and then went with him to Baxter Springs, where Parham preached the Apostolic Faith camp meeting. Opperman probably informed Parham of the developments in Zion, including the financial difficulties, the deposing of Dowie, and the spiritual crisis among the people. Of course, some of the information had appeared in newspapers across the nation. At the same time, he

D. C. O. Opperman

began writing to the overseers and his colleagues in Zion about Parham and the baptism of the Holy Ghost, although he had not yet received the Holy Ghost.

From Baxter Springs, Opperman went to Kansas City,

Missouri, where he stayed five weeks preaching at the Zion branch and telling them about the baptism of the Holy Ghost. Before he returned to San Antonio, he briefly visited Zion City, and again shared with the people the story of Charles Parham and the outpouring of the Holy Ghost.

In Zion Opperman discovered five men who apparently had been stirred by the Pentecostal experience of Mrs. Waldron, Mrs. Hall, and Louise Albach in 1904. Recently they had also heard about the revival at the Azusa Street Mission in Los Angeles. For several months these men had been quietly praying regularly together at the Elijah Hospice, of which one was the manager. When Opperman told them about Parham, they wrote Parham and urged him to come to Zion.

In the summer of 1906, Parham began receiving letters from Seymour, requesting him to come to Los Angeles to help him in the revival. He had planned to go to Los Angeles in the fall, but learning about Zion, he pondered whether he should go to Zion immediately. When he received the letter from the five men, he felt that God told him to go to Zion before going to Los Angeles.

The Revival Begins in Zion

When Parham arrived in Zion on September 20, he went immediately to the Elijah Hospice and was given a room by the manager, George A. Rogers, one of the five men who had invited him to come to Zion. That same evening, Parham held a meeting that had been quietly arranged in one of the rooms made available by Rogers. The next evening two rooms were needed and people also filled the hall. The third day, Parham began holding three meetings each day to accommodate the crowds that continued to increase.

On September 26, *The Daily Sun*, a newspaper of Waukegan, a nearby town, reported that Parham had "attracted several hundred followers," and Voliva was quoted as saying, "This man is winning some of our most faithful people."

Voliva was able to force Parham from the Elijah Hospice since it was under his control, and he would not allow Parham to use any public building in the city. But one family opened their private home to Parham to hold meetings. *The Daily Sun* reported that "the house was crowded and the congregation covered the lawn" and noted that "some of the prominent elders" of Zion had accepted Parham's Pentecostal message. This newspaper also noted that A. F. Lee, who had converted to Parham's Pentecostal view, had resigned his position as general ecclesiastical secretary of the church.

Other homes were subsequently opened until there were daily and evening meetings in six to eight homes. Parham's followers in Zion soon numbered in the hundreds, many of whom received the baptism of the Holy Ghost. On October 15, *The Daily Gazette* reported that Parham to this point had gained two hundred followers, but the work was growing so fast that he had sent to Kansas for two of his coworkers, Mabel Smith and Jessie Brown. With their coming the work multiplied several times.

On October 18, 1906, three prominent Zion members received the Holy Ghost: Marie E. Burgess, Fred F. Bosworth, and Jean Campbell. All three would become important in the Pentecostal movement. With the arrival of Mabel Smith and Jessie Brown, and since the revival was gaining strength, Parham felt that he should go to Los Angeles to assist Seymour, who had mentioned some manifestations in the Azusa Street revival and needed to know if they were of God.

Parham knew that he would need to return to Zion as soon as possible, and so his trip to Los Angeles would necessarily be short. But he did not anticipate that his visit to the Azusa Street Mission would result in the first division in the Apostolic Faith movement.

CHAPTER SIX

DIVISION AT AZUSA

William Seymour had learned that Charles Parham was issuing ministerial credentials, so he wrote W. F. Carothers, requesting a ministerial license in Parham's Apostolic Faith movement. Parham approved, and in July 1906, Seymour became a licensed minister with the movement.

During the August 1906 Apostolic Faith meeting in Houston, Lucy Farrow, who had gone to Los Angeles to assist Seymour in igniting the outpouring of the Spirit in that city, returned to Houston on her way to Liberia, West Africa. Speaking in the Brunner tabernacle, she related the wonderful events at the revival at Azusa Street. Her report stirred Anna Hall, Mr. and Mrs. Walter Oyler, and their son Mahlon to go to Los Angeles to assist in the revival. Parham raised funds to pay the train fare for Anna Hall, who left immediately for the city. A short time later the Oylers went.

From Houston, Farrow went to her hometown, Norfolk, Virginia, where she introduced the Pentecostal experience to the city, and about two hundred people received the Holy Ghost. In late December she sailed to Liberia, held meetings in Johnston (a suburb of Monrovia in which many former slaves from America had settled), and reported that about fifteen Liberians had received the Holy Ghost. Farrow had been born into slavery, and her interest in Liberia, and in particular the area of Johnston, may have been personal, for it is possible that she had friends and even relatives who were among those who had returned to Africa in 1847 to establish the nation of Liberia. She only stayed seven months in Liberia, and in July 1907 she returned to Los Angeles, where she lived the rest of her life in a cottage behind the Azusa Street Mission.

It should be noted that Farrow, who was a niece of the famous Frederick Douglass, played a key and remarkable role in the Azusa Street Mission, in that she was the link that brought Seymour into the Apostolic Faith movement and was an important instrument that God used to spark the revival in Los Angeles.

Division in the Apostolic Faith Movement

In August 1906, while Parham was still in Houston, he received a letter from Seymour, requesting him to come to Los Angeles to help him in the Pentecostal outpouring at the Azusa Street Mission. Parham immediately made plans to go to Los Angeles in mid-September after leading two camp meetings that were to be held in early September in Kansas.

Parham sent word, perhaps by Anna Hall, that he would soon visit Los Angeles. In a letter to Parham dated August 27, 1906, Seymour wrote that Hall had arrived and that they were making plans for Parham to hold a citywide revival, bringing together all the Pentecostal missions in the city. He requested the date when Parham would arrive in Los Angeles so that he could secure a large building for the meeting. The letter contained a glowing report of the Azusa Street revival and an expectation that Parham's ministry would bring a fresh outpouring of the Spirit that would "shake this city once more."

During the camp meetings in Kansas, D. C. O. Opperman, who had accompanied Parham, kept him abreast of the events in Zion City. As mentioned above, when Parham received the invitation from the five men from Zion to bring the Pentecostal message to the city, he decided to go to Zion before his trip to Los Angeles. In October, after several remarkable weeks of revival there, Parham handed the leadership over to others and hurried to Los Angeles.

The Azusa Street Mission and the Apostolic Faith Movement

Until November 1906, the entire Apostolic Faith movement, which had spread in Kansas, Missouri, Oklahoma, Texas, California, Illinois, and other states, remained unified under Parham's leadership. With his trip to Los Angeles, this unity was fractured when a dispute erupted between him and Seymour. Neither man wanted or expected this dispute that suddenly changed their relationship and produced the first open schism in the movement.

Before Parham arrived in Los Angeles, Seymour had announced that Parham was coming and referred to him as the founder and projector of the Apostolic Faith movement. On the front page of the first issue of *The Apostolic Faith* published in Los Angeles (September 1906), Seymour referred to events leading to the outpouring of the Holy

67

Ghost in Los Angeles during a cottage prayer meeting on Bonnie Brae Street. Following this review was a report of Parham's letter in which he wrote Seymour of his plans to be in Los Angeles by September 15. In the letter, Parham wrote, "I rejoice in God over you all, my children, though I have never seen you; but . . . we are baptized by one Spirit into one body." He also promised to conduct a grand meeting of all the Apostolic Faith believers in the city.

On the same page appears a brief report on the beginning of the Pentecostal revival under the leadership of Parham in Topeka, Kansas, in 1901. It also mentions the rapid growth of the movement during the next five years, noting that "something like 13,000 people have received the gospel." Moreover, the article places the revival in Los Angeles in Parham's Apostolic Faith movement.

In the second issue of *The Apostolic Faith* (October 1906), a front-page article again gives the history of the Pentecostal movement, noting that it began in Topeka on January 1, 1901, and then ends by noting that the people at the Azusa Street Mission were expecting "Bro. Parham to visit Los Angeles in a few days and for a mightier tide of salvation to break out."

In the same issue, Parham's role in founding the Apostolic Faith movement and his current leadership are acknowledged: "Before another issue of this paper we look for Bro. Parham in Los Angeles, a brother who is full of divine love and whom the Lord raised up five years ago to spread this truth. He, with other workers, will hold union revival meetings in Los Angeles . . . and shall appoint workers to fill the calls that shall come in." When Parham arrived at the Azusa Street Mission in October, Seymour introduced him as his father in the Lord.

The Cause of the Schism

Apparently the schism was over leadership and was ignited when Parham set about to correct certain practices that he regarded as deceptive satanic influences that would, if unchecked, destroy the revival. Parham understood that Seymour had wanted him to evaluate certain manifestations that were taking place and correct them if he regarded them as false spiritual practices. He had been informed about the practices, for he later wrote, "I hurried to Los Angeles, and to my surprise and astonishment I found conditions even worse than I had anticipated. Brother Seymour came to me helpless; he said he could not stem the tide that had arisen. I sat on the platform in Azusa Street Mission, and saw the manifestations of the flesh, spiritualistic controls, saw people practicing hypnotism at the altar over candidates seeking the baptism; though many were receiving the real baptism of the Holy Ghost."

After Parham had preached only two or three times at the Azusa Street Mission, two elders informed him that he was not wanted and not to come back. Of course, these elders were acting with the approval of Seymour.

Leaving the Azusa Street Mission, Parham gathered workers who had come from Texas and began meetings in the Women's Christian Temperance Union building on Broadway and Temple Streets. He drew large crowds and reported that "marvelous healings took place and between two and three hundred who had been possessed of awful fits and spasm and controls in the Azusa Street work were delivered and received the real Pentecost teachings and many spake with other tongues."

Parham attributed the cause of the division to Seymour's desire for leadership recognition. Parham's wife wrote, "W. J. Seymour, in his first paper gave a true account of the origin of the work, but after he failed to receive the message Mr. Parham brought, he was possessed with a spirit of leadership and sought to prove that Azusa St. Mission was where the baptism of the Holy Ghost first fell."

On his part, Seymour immediately established the Pacific Apostolic Faith movement to distinguish the Azusa Street Mission from Parham's Apostolic Faith movement. The new name appeared in the November 1906 issue of *The Apostolic Faith.* In the December issue of the paper, the opening article on the front page contains statements aimed at Parham's official title and renounces any leadership he may have had over the Azusa Street Mission: "The Lord was the founder and He is the Projector of this movement. . . . There is no pope, Dowieism, or Sanfordism, but we all little children knowing only Jesus and Him crucified. . . . Brother Seymour is simply a humble pastor of the flock."

Frank Bartleman, who disliked any form of church organization, denounced Parham's visit as an attempt to take over the work in Los Angeles: "An earlier work in Texas later tried to gather in the Pentecostal missions on the Pacific Coast, and Los Angeles, but also failed. Why should they claim authority over us? We had prayed down our own revival."

CHAPTER SEVEN

THE DECLINE OF PARHAM AND SEYMOUR

After Parham returned from Los Angeles in December 1906, he moved his family from southeastern Kansas to Zion, Illinois, arriving in Zion in time to celebrate the New Year's Day with his followers in the city. While Parham was in Los Angeles, his followers in Zion erected a large tent for services, a tent that would seat about two thousand people. A local newspaper reported that the tent was full for the New Year's Eve service and that people had come from about thirty states to attend the meeting. The newspaper also reported that Parham preached two hours on the baptism of the Holy Ghost.

During the two months Parham was away, many others in Zion had received the Holy Ghost, resulting in about twenty percent of the population becoming Pentecostal. Yet the revival in the city and among Zion followers across North America and around the world had only begun. We should emphasize that the newspaper article stated that people had come from about thirty states to the tent services. This points not only to the spread of the Zion movement in North America but also to the widespread interest among Zion followers in Parham's message of the baptism of the Holy Ghost.

Parham's Trip to Eastern States and Canada

After the New Year celebration, Parham continued to preach and teach for four days to large crowds in the tent. He also opened a Bible training school in the city, commissioned several workers, and sent some of these workers to cities in Canada and in eastern states of the United States. During the second week of January 1907, Parham left his family in Zion to take the Pentecostal message to several cities not only in the East, but also to Toronto, Ontario, Canada.

His first stop was Cleveland, Ohio, where he visited a Quaker church and Bible school, staying only a day and night. He then went to Toledo, Ohio, where he preached about the baptism of the Holy Ghost to a mixed congregation of several denominations. He left the results of his preaching as an "extension of the work" under the leadership of his sister-in-law, Lillian Thistlethwaite.

He next went to Toronto, arriving in the city on Sunday, January 13. He quickly found the place of the Zion gathering, whose leader, Eugene Brooks, invited him to preach. Brooks also arranged for Parham to conduct a union meeting downtown in Wolesley Hall.

For the next three weeks, Parham held two services each day in the hall. Neither Brooks nor his wife had received the Holy Ghost, but after becoming convinced of Parham's message, they severed their relationship with Dowie's Zion movement and began seeking God for the baptism of the Holy Ghost. Later, Parham persuaded Mr.

and Mrs. Henry W. Robinson from Zion to move to Toronto to assist Brooks.

In April, after Parham left Toronto, Mrs. Brooks received the Holy Ghost, but Pastor Brooks did not receive the Holy Ghost until the winter of 1908. The influence of the ministries of the Brookses and the Robinsons brought many other Zion ministers into the Pentecostal movement.

From Toronto, Parham went to Boston, where he ministered to a congregation that had left the local Zion gathering to seek the baptism of the Holy Ghost. Apparently these people had heard about the outpouring of the Spirit in Zion and in Los Angeles. Some of them had accepted the Pentecostal message, resulting in a division in the Zion gathering. This was also happening in the Zion gatherings in other cities in North America, resulting in many Zion ministers and believers entering the Pentecostal movement.

After preaching in Boston for three weeks, Parham went to New York City to assist Marie Burgess and Jean Campbell, whom he had sent from Zion City to start a mission in this city. The two ladies secured Volunteer Hall on Forty-Second Street, in which Parham conducted services for two weeks.

On March 9, Dowie died after a long and painful illness. His death may have prompted Parham to return to Zion sooner than he had planned, but before returning to Zion, Parham stopped in Cleveland, where he visited the former Zion gathering and found the people in a Pentecostal revival.

Parham returned to Zion on March 23. After conducting services for four days, he moved his family back

to southeastern Kansas and then quickly went to Orchard
for the annual Easter services held there.

Parham's ministry in Zion gatherings and in Zion City
virtually ended in April 1907. Although he returned to
hold meetings in Zion during 1914 and 1915, the results
were meager. It is what he accomplished in the few
months in 1906 in Zion that made a lasting impact on the
Pentecostal movement. Not only were thousands of lay
members added to the Pentecostal movement, but many
capable ministers were also added who would become
prominent Pentecostal evangelists, pastors, and organizational leaders.

The Leadership of Charles Parham

For the first six years of the Pentecostal revival,
Parham was the recognized leader of the movement. To
Parham we must give credit for recovering and promoting
the biblical doctrine that speaking in tongues is the evidence or sign of the baptism of the Holy Ghost. Since this
doctrine was vital not only to the Pentecostal outpouring
in Topeka but also to the Pentecostal revival that followed, it is proper to recognize Parham as the founder of
the Pentecostal movement. This recognition is also based
on his leadership that spearheaded and guided the revival
from its inception in January 1901 until it grew into a
movement by the fall of 1906.

Until the last months of 1906, Parham was the
unchallenged leader of the movement, both in the
Midwest and at the Azusa Street Mission. However, as we
noted earlier, when he visited the Azusa Street Mission in
late October 1906, Seymour and the mission elders
rejected Parham's leadership after he condemned certain

physical displays that he regarded as fanatical, fleshly, and demonic.

The rejection of his leadership by the Azusa Street Mission was the first challenge to Parham's leadership, but events in the Midwest indicated that his leadership role was in trouble in the heartland of the movement.

By the end of 1906, rumors were being circulated about Parham's leadership and character. Parham's wife, Sarah, wrote that during the early months of 1907 they were aware that "many scandalous reports were being scattered and published" against Parham. She related that two preachers came to her home to talk to her about the substance of these "evil reports," but she refused to answer any questions or make any comment. She received a letter after their visit in which they reiterated "all manner of evil spoken falsely against Mr. Parham" and then offered to provide for her and her children since they didn't want them to suffer.

Even some of Parham's close followers and friends were turning against him. Sarah wrote that while Parham was in New York "the fight still raged bitterly against him, which was also joined by our friends who had turned against him because he refused to organize."

When Parham returned from Los Angeles to Zion, he published his resignation of the office of projector of the movement. In the January 1907 issue of *Apostolic Faith* (published in Zion), he wrote, "In resigning my position as Projector of the Apostolic Faith Movement, I simply followed a well considered plan of mine, made years ago, never to receive honor of men, or to establish a new church. I was called a pope, a Dowie, etc., and every-where looked upon as a leader or a would-be leader and proselyter. These designations have always been an abomination to me and since God has given almost universal light to the world on Pentecost there is no further need of my holding the official leadership of the Apostolic Faith Movement."

Parham's resignation came as a surprise to many of his followers, and some, such as Howard Goss, protested to him for resigning. In spite of his published resignation, Parham continued to be recognized as the leader of the movement in the Midwest until July 1907 when he was arrested in San Antonio on a charge of sodomy. Although the charge was dropped without prosecution, most of his followers judged him guilty and separated their ministry from him. For a short time, they continued to use the name Apostolic Faith, but they soon chose the name Pentecostal so as not to be identified with Parham.

After July 1907, and until his death in January 1929, Parham refused to organize his remaining followers, which was only a tiny segment (only a few thousand) of the movement he founded, but he held them together by his charisma and leadership skills.

The Contribution of Charles Parham

Parham's recovery of the biblical doctrine of speaking in tongues as the physical sign of the baptism of the Holy Ghost and his successful ministry in Kansas, Texas, and especially in Zion, Illinois, sparked revivals that produced the Apostolic Faith movement. This loose organization held the mushrooming movement together during 1905 and 1906 as it spread throughout Kansas, Missouri, Texas, Illinois, and through Seymour into California.

Although it was the Azusa Street revival under the

leadership of Seymour that sparked the fledgling Pentecostal revival into becoming a worldwide movement, Parham laid the necessary theological foundation for the movement to become worldwide.

The Decline of the Leadership Role of William Joseph Seymour

Surprisingly, Seymour's own ministry, after the glorious revival at the Azusa Street Mission, had all but ended in 1909. With the focus of the revival shifting to other missions along the West Coast and to several cities in the Midwest, the Azusa Street Mission diminished to become only a small, mostly black, congregation. Consequently, Seymour's national leadership role also faded. For the next few years, Seymour and a small group of workers held meetings in a few cities in North America, but soon his ministry was focused on the small congregation that remained at the Azusa Street Mission. The Pacific Apostolic Faith movement, which he had founded to distinguish his group from Parham and to organize the Pentecostals on the West Coast, was no longer needed or relevant.

Seymour also lost his leadership role for other reasons, one of which was that he turned from the foundational Pentecostal teaching that speaking in tongues is the evidence or sign of the baptism of the Holy Ghost; instead, he regarded tongues as only one of the spiritual gifts. For this reason, as well as others, most Pentecostals left the Azusa Street Mission to attend other Pentecostal missions in Los Angeles. Seymour attributed his diminished role and small congregation to racial prejudice since most white Pentecostals had left; however, while prejudice may have been responsible in part, other factors must also be considered.

After Seymour's death in 1922, his wife, Jennie Moore, became the pastor of the Azusa Street Mission. By this time the congregation consisted of only a handful of people. In 1931 the building burned to the ground. In 1936, after suffering from failing health, Jennie Moore died. In 1936, the Azusa Street property was lost through foreclosure.

The Contribution of William Seymour

The Azusa Street revival under the leadership of Seymour propelled the Pentecostal message across the United States and around the world. Its impact was worldwide, converting missionaries of many denominations to Pentecostalism and inspiring people to go as missionaries to nations around the globe. Moreover, the Azusa Street revival left us a touchstone of Pentecostal revivalism that still inspires today.

The Shift to New Leadership

In the spring of 1906 Parham had begun his first efforts to organize the Apostolic Faith movement by issuing ministerial credentials to workers and appointing various leaders. By the fall of 1906, W. F. Carothers, Howard Goss, and Seymour were the only recognized national Pentecostal leaders under the general leadership of Parham. But the wave of new converts during 1906 through 1908 brought into the movement scores of others who would become leaders in the mushrooming movement. Since most of these emerging leaders were already ministers, pastors, evangelists, and denominational leaders, they already had leadership experience and respect among groups of people.

By 1909, the national leadership of Parham and Seymour had faded into the background. Carothers still exerted some influence from Houston, and Goss remained a respected leader in the Midwest. From the Zion movement, under the ministry of Parham and his followers, came other leaders such D. C. O. Opperman, L. C. Hall, Fred F. Bosworth, John G. Lake, Cyrus B. Fockler, Marie E. Burgess, Martha Wing Robinson, Eugene Brooks, Fred Vogler, William Hamner Piper, and others.

Out of the revival at the Azusa Street Mission came Frank Bartleman, Glenn Cook, Florence Crawford, Elmer K. Fisher, Harry Morse, Thomas Hezmalhalch, and a host of others. Among those going to the Azusa Street Mission to receive the Holy Ghost were William Durham and Charles Harrison Mason. Others who came into the Pentecostal experience through ministers from the Azusa Street Mission include Frank Ewart, G. T. Haywood, Joseph Roswell Flower, E. N. Bell, H. G. Rodgers, A. H. Argue, Andrew D. Urshan, George T. Studd, R. E. McAlister, Frank Small, Thomas Barratt, and T. K. Leonard—to name only a few of the Pentecostal leaders who came out of this revival.

CHAPTER EIGHT

THE SPREADING REVIVAL

The year of 1906 may have witnessed the events that made the Pentecostal revival a worldwide reality. In that year, the Pentecostal message gained a significant beachhead in the Midwest, especially in Texas and Illinois, under the leadership of Charles Parham. The revival in the Azusa Street Mission under the leadership of William Seymour not only impacted the city of Los Angeles but also established Pentecostal missions in California from San Diego to Oakland and reached Seattle, Washington, and crossed the border into Canada. Missionaries, both foreign and home, began leaving Los Angeles to spread the revival across North America and around the world. By the beginning of 1907, the revival was poised to become a major worldwide movement.

Glenn A. Cook and the Revival in Indiana

Glenn Cook, a Baptist who had converted to become a minister in the Holiness movement, was working at a daily newspaper in Los Angeles in April 1906 when

Seymour began services in the Azusa Street Mission. Out of curiosity, Cook visited the mission in late April, but the meeting did not impress him. He dismissed the teaching on tongues as heresy. However, after "Pentecost came to the place, and many began to speak in tongues," he began attending regularly and soon received the Holy Ghost.

In the November 1906 issue of *The Apostolic Faith*, Cook wrote that after seeking the baptism at the Azusa Street Mission over a period of five weeks, he received the Holy Ghost. He then quit his job at the newspaper and began working full time with Seymour at the Azusa Street Mission. Among other duties, he handled the mission's finances and correspondence and assisted in the publication of *The Apostolic Faith*.

On December 4 he left Los Angeles to take the message of Pentecost to his acquaintances and others in Indianapolis, Indiana, where he had lived before moving to California. About a week later he arrived in Lamont, Oklahoma, where he conducted services among a group of Holiness people. By the first week of January 1907, a number of people had received the Holy Ghost, but Oklahoma was not his destination nor was it to be the site of his most important revival.

On January 14, Cook left Oklahoma, spent a couple of days in Chicago, and arrived in Indianapolis on Friday, January 18. On Sunday he gave his testimony during the afternoon service to the Christian and Missionary Alliance congregation pastored by George N. Eldridge. The next day, January 21, he reported that "quite a number here are seeking the baptism" (*The Apostolic Faith*, January 1907, 1). However, Eldridge, who was out of town when Cook testified, returned and denounced Cook's teaching and closed the church to further prayer meetings. It was troublesome to find another meeting place, but eventually Cook secured a room upstairs at 1111 Shelby Street.

Before Cook returned to Los Angeles in March, he went to Memphis, Tennessee, where he preached in the Church of God in Christ, whose pastor, Charles Harrison Mason, and two of his assistant ministers had gone to Los Angeles to receive the Holy Ghost at the Azusa Street Mission. Several of the people in this black Holiness church received the Holy Ghost in the few days Cook was there.

After Cook returned to Los Angeles, he reported on March 20 that in Indianapolis "many received the baptism with the Holy Ghost and are speaking with tongues. They came from different parts of Indiana and are now going forth to spread the good news" (*The Apostolic Faith*, February-March 1907, 3). He also predicted that Indianapolis "will be a great center of power, being an interurban railway center like Los Angeles."

After Cook left Indianapolis, Tom Hezmalhalch, an evangelist also from Azusa Street, arrived with a group of workers to guide the young Pentecostal revival. By April the Pentecostals began holding services downtown in Murphy League Hall at the corner of New York and Alabama. On April 20, Hezmalhalch reported that many others were receiving the Holy Ghost in spite of unfavorable articles in the newspapers. From his report we learn that the services were interracial and growing (*The Apostolic Faith*, April 1907, 1.)

An article in the *Indianapolis Morning Star* (April 27,

1907) confirmed that crowds were attending the Pentecostal meeting: "Murphy League Hall was crowded last night. The meetings, being conducted by Apostolic Christians, speakers of strange tongues, are approaching their acme of wild enthusiasm. Odd demonstrations, strange words, sidewalk arguments, gifts to brothers and sisters, with something decidedly now relative to the doctrinal experience of converts marked last evening's gathering."

In Los Angeles, Cook encouraged Henry Prentiss, a black minister in the Azusa Street Mission, to go to Indianapolis and minister. Prentiss arrived in the city in 1908 and opened a mission on West Michigan Street in a building used for a tin shop. It was in this building that G. T. Haywood received the Holy Ghost. Haywood became the assistant pastor, and when Prentiss left the city in 1909, he became the pastor. Under Haywood's ministry, the mission grew to become one of the largest and most influential churches in the Pentecostal movement. It also became a strong center for Oneness Pentecostals.

A Brief Recap

The Pentecostal revival in the twentieth century began among people in the Holiness movement in North America. Charles Parham had become a part of the Holiness movement before the outpouring of the Holy Ghost occurred in Topeka in 1901. Moreover, most of the students attending the Bible school he had opened in Topeka in October 1900 had come from Holiness missions and churches, and the course of study was centered on standard Holiness teachings. Since the outpouring of the Spirit occurred among Holiness people, it would seem that Parham would have quick success among Holiness churches. But this was not the case. For two years, the same group of Pentecostals struggled, but survived.

Even after the great revival of 1903-1904 in Galena, Kansas, the Apostolic Faith movement had less than two thousand people and was mostly confined to a relatively small area in Kansas, Missouri, and Arkansas. For the most part, the Apostolic Faith movement was unknown and unnoticed by the Holiness movement.

A change began, however, when Parham took the Pentecostal message to Texas in the spring of 1905. The revival in the small town of Orchard soon spread to the Brunner Holiness church in Houston. This church, with its pastor, W. F. Carothers, soon became a center of the Apostolic Faith movement in Texas. In Houston, Parham convinced Lucy Farrow and William Seymour, both Holiness ministers, of the truth of the Pentecostal message, and Farrow received the Holy Ghost in the summer of 1905.

In the spring of 1906, Parham met D. C. O. Opperman, a minister from Zion, Illinois, who had been ordained into the ministry by John Alexander Dowie. Most of Dowie's doctrines agreed with the Holiness movement. After Opperman accepted the Pentecostal message, he opened the door for Parham to hold a revival in Zion in which about two thousand people came into Pentecostalism. Moreover, most ministers and leaders in Zion became Pentecostal, and their leadership skills would contribute to the shaping and spread of Pentecostalism in the decades following. But the revival among the Zionist followers in the fall of 1906 was to be Parham's greatest and last success in bringing Holiness people, both laity and ministers, into the Pentecostal experience.

From Azusa Street Mission
across North America

While Parham's success among Holiness people was small, Seymour and the Azusa Street revival found a harvest field for the Pentecostal message. Although many unchurched people made their way to the Azusa Street Mission to receive the Holy Ghost, records indicate that most people came from Holiness churches. For example, the October 1906 issue of *The Apostolic Faith* reports that four Holiness preachers had received the Holy Ghost. One of these preachers, William Pendleton, brought his entire congregation into the Pentecostal experience.

This was not an isolated event. Frank Bartleman wrote that "Holiness meetings, tents, and missions began to close up for lack of attendance. Their people were at 'Azusa.' Brother and Sister A. G. Garr closed the 'Burning Bush' hall, came to 'Azusa,' and received the Holy Ghost."

Bartleman, as mentioned earlier, remarked that "one reason for the depth of the work at Azusa was the fact that the workers were not novices. They were largely called and prepared for years, from the Holiness ranks, and from the mission field, etc. . . . They were largely seasoned veterans." Almost every early issue of *The Apostolic Faith* recorded ministers and laity from the Holiness movement coming into Pentecostalism. In October 1906, *The Apostolic Faith* listed at least eight other Pentecostal missions in the Los Angeles area; some of these Pentecostal missions had been Holiness missions.

Indeed, the rapid spread of Pentecostalism among Holiness groups in Los Angeles soon ignited Pentecostal revivals in Holiness churches and missions across North

America and even to nations around the world. By the fall of 1906, workers at the Azusa Street Mission were traveling to other cities in California, Oregon, and Washington, spreading Pentecostalism to Long Beach, Clearwater, San Diego, Oakland, Fresno, San Jose, Stockton, Whittier, Santa Rosa, and other cities in California, to Portland and Salem in Oregon, and to Seattle and Spokane in Washington. In some of these cities, entire Holiness churches became Pentecostal.

But the revival was greater than the West Coast. In late 1906, a few workers at the Azusa Street Mission left Los Angeles to speed Pentecostalism in the Midwest, East, and South.

Ivey Campbell and the Revival in Ohio

While visiting Los Angeles, Ivey Campbell attended the meetings at the Azusa Street Mission, received the Holy Ghost, and became a volunteer worker at the mission. But in the winter of 1906, she felt a burden to carry the Pentecostal experience she received at the Azusa Street Mission to her home in Ohio.

In October or November, Campbell wrote to Claude A. McKinley, pastor of the Union Gospel Mission in Akron, to tell him of the happenings in the revival in Los Angeles. She perhaps knew McKinley and wanted to know if he had any interest in learning about the outpouring of the Spirit. An announcement in the December 1906 issue of *The Apostolic Faith* informs us that she and others left Los Angeles "for points in Ohio."

Campbell arrived in East Liverpool on December 1; however, she stayed there only a few days before going to Akron. She learned that people in the Union Gospel

Mission had been praying and seeking for an outpouring of the Spirit. McKinley welcomed her and opened the church to her for a Pentecostal revival, which began on December 5.

By December 27 many people in the church had received the Holy Ghost. The altar overflowed with seekers in almost every service. Then in January 1907 they heard news that an outpouring was happening in Pittsburgh, Pennsylvania. Campbell wrote, "God is visiting every hungry town and city that will receive him." After the revival in Akron, Campbell held revivals in Cleveland and in Pittsburgh and Springboro, Pennsylvania.

Levi R. Lupton, a minister affiliated with the Society of Friends (Quakers) and head of the Missionary Faith Home in Alliance, Ohio, attended the revival services in Akron. After he returned to Alliance, he received the baptism of the Holy Ghost on December 30. Consequently, the district meeting of Friends held in February dismissed him from their ministry.

In June, Campbell and McKinley worked with Lupton to hold a Pentecostal camp meeting hosted by Lupton's faith home in Alliance. Several prominent Pentecostal ministers participated in the camp meeting, including Frank Bartleman. This camp meeting was a key in the spread of the Pentecostal revival into the Northeast and especially among the Christian and Missionary Alliance churches in Ohio.

Gaston Barnabas Cashwell and the Revival in the South

Frank Bartleman wrote scores of articles about the outpouring of the Spirit during the early months of the revival in Los Angeles, which were published in Holiness magazines that circulated throughout the East and South. While it is difficult to assess the role that Bartleman's writings played in spreading Pentecostal revival, it was significant. Pentecostal historian Vinson Synan wrote, "It is probable that without [Bartleman's] reporting, the Pentecostal movement would not have spread so quickly and so far as it did." This was especially true of the revival among the Holiness groups in the South and the Christian and Missionary Alliance.

In late October 1906, or perhaps in the first of November, Gaston Barnabas Cashwell, in Dunn, North Carolina, read some articles by Bartleman on the revival at Azusa. Cashwell had been a Holiness preacher for nine years, but he later wrote, "My soul began to hunger and thirst for the fullness of God." Borrowing money for train fare, he traveled the three thousand miles to Los Angeles. After praying for the baptism of the Spirit for about a week at the Azusa Street Mission, in one service he suddenly began speaking in tongues.

Although he wanted to return to his home, he had no money for train fare. However, the Azusa Street Mission took up an offering and was able not only to pay his train fare but also to buy him a new suit. Cashwell arrived in Dunn in about the middle of December. He preached a few services in two Holiness churches near Dunn and reported that two people received the Holy Ghost in these services. Near the end of December, he rented a large barn-like building in Dunn that was used as a tobacco warehouse and prepared it for a Pentecostal meeting. One of the greatest of Pentecostal revivals began in this building on December 31, 1906. Cashwell invited all the ministers of three Holiness organizations to attend the meeting: the Fire-Baptized Holiness Church, the Pentecostal Holiness Church, and the Free Will Baptist Church. Most of them attended the revival. From the first evening, the services were overwhelming. Thousands of Holiness people, including most of the ministers from the Holiness churches, crowded into the building to hear about the Pentecostal outpouring. Almost immediately people began receiving the Holy Ghost. By January 2, 1907, ten people had received the Holy Ghost; five of them were preachers.

The meeting in Dunn lasted for about a month, in which time hundreds of people received the Holy Ghost, including many ministers of the Fire-Baptized Holiness Church and the Pentecostal Holiness Church. People came not only from North Carolina but also from South Carolina, Georgia, Florida, and Alabama. Out of this revival, three Holiness organizations—the Fire-Baptized Holiness Church, the Pentecostal Holiness Church, and the Free Will Baptist Church—eventually came into the Pentecostal movement. After this revival Cashwell evangelized in Holiness churches in the Southeast and witnessed thousands joining the Pentecostal movement. For this he is known as the Pentecostal Apostle to the South.

Shortly after the meeting in Dunn ended in early February, Cashwell held a meeting in Bonneau, South Carolina, in which twenty-three received the Holy Ghost, including an evangelist of the Methodist Episcopal Church. From Bonneau, he held a meeting in Taccoa, Georgia, where J. H. King, the general overseer of the Fire-Baptized Holiness Church, received the Holy Ghost along with many others. Leaving Taccoa, Cashwell preached in Alvin, South

Carolina, where about twenty more people received the Holy Ghost, including F. M. Britton, a leader of the Fire-Baptized Holiness Church in North Carolina who became a well-known pioneer Pentecostal evangelist. Later, in a meeting in Birmingham, Alabama, M. M. Pinson and H. G. Rodgers, both future Pentecostal leaders, received the Holy Ghost.

Cashwell continued to evangelize throughout the South until 1909, bringing thousands of Holiness people and at least three Holiness organizations into the Pentecostal movement.

THE FIRE CONTINUES TO SPREAD

It is amazing how quickly the revival spread from the Azusa Street Mission to other areas in the short time from the revival's beginning in April 1906 until the end of that year. By December 1906 news of the Azusa Street revival was even reaching missionaries in foreign nations, primarily through *The Apostolic Faith* and personal letters. Moreover, by the end of December, several people had gone from the Azusa Street Mission to work as missionaries in foreign fields: G. W. Batman, his wife, Daisy, and their three small children; Lucy Farrow; Thomas P. Mahler; Robert Shideler and his wife; Julia Hutchins, her husband, and her niece, Leila McKinney. All of these went to Africa. Lucy Leatherman and Louise Condit went to Jerusalem and the Middle East. A. G. Garr and his wife went to India. Eric Hollingsworth and his wife and Andrew Johnson went to Sweden. Although some of these missionaries did not arrive in the country of their calling until 1907, all of them had left Los Angeles by the end of December 1906.

It is more than remarkable that this fervent evangelistic effort and missionary activity emerged out of the Azusa Street Mission when the core membership of the mission was probably no more than fifty to seventy people; however, the attendance often reached more than three hundred people, an overflowing crowd for the building. In the September 1906 issue of *The Apostolic Faith*, it was reported that "about a dozen full-time workers" were at the Azusa Street Mission. It seems incredible that such a small group working in the old barn-like building on Azusa Street could be the spark that turned the Pentecostal revival into a worldwide movement.

Florence Louise Crawford

In her testimony published in *The Apostolic Faith*, Florence Crawford wrote that she came from a family of infidels and "everything that would drive me from God." She, nevertheless, had a conversion experience in a Holiness church and then received the Holy Ghost at the Azusa Street Mission, where she soon became one of the leaders at the mission.

After Seymour and the Azusa Street Mission separated from Parham, Seymour formed the Pacific Apostolic Faith movement, in which Crawford served as one of the twelve members on the credential committee. This committee issued ministerial credentials to evangelists and missionaries. Crawford also assisted in the publication of *The Apostolic Faith*.

When an evangelistic band of workers went from the Azusa Street Mission in the summer of 1906 to hold a meeting in Oakland, California, Crawford joined them. Others in the band were G. W. Evans and his wife;

Thomas Junk and his wife, Ophelia Wiley; and Lulu Miller. Apparently a Brother Manley, who lived in Oakland and was the editor of *Household of God*, a Holiness paper, persuaded the workers to go to Oakland and helped organize the meeting. In the September 1906 issue of *The Apostolic Faith*, G. W. Evans reported on the Oakland meetings, stating that hundreds of people had been seeking God at the altar, thirty people had received the Holy Ghost, and many people had been healed. In a later report in the October issue, the number of people receiving the Holy Ghost had increased to sixty-five.

In the same October issue, Crawford expressed her desire to be more involved in evangelistic work. She wrote, "There is no place on earth so dear to me than this place; but I must go out and tell this story."

By December 1906 Crawford had begun her evangelistic ministry into the Pacific Northwest. In early December she held cottage meetings in San Francisco, in which several people received the Holy Ghost, including at least one preacher. From San Francisco she went to Salem, Oregon, where M. L. Ryan, the editor of *Light*, a Holiness paper, came into the Pentecostal movement and converted his paper into a Pentecostal publication. Crawford soon moved to Portland, Oregon, arriving in the city on December 25. She began conducting service in a Holiness mission that was turned over to her.

It was in Portland that Crawford found her greatest success, and she made the city the center of her ministry in the Pacific Northwest. From her base in Portland, she established missions in several cities, including Salem, Oregon; Seattle, Washington; Minneapolis, Minnesota; and Winnipeg, Manitoba, Canada, all of which looked to her for leadership. In early 1907 she formed a loose organization of these missions in the Northwest, adopting the name Apostolic Faith Mission (Portland, Oregon). Later the name of the organization was changed to the Apostolic Faith Church.

One of the ministers from Los Angeles who visited Crawford's mission in Portland during May 1907 was Henry Prentiss, the minister who later opened the mission in Indianapolis that ultimately became one of the largest Oneness Pentecostal churches under the leadership of G. T. Haywood.

Although Crawford had formed a loose association of missions in the Northwest, she continued to work with Seymour at the Azusa Street Mission until May 1908 when she separated from his work. The reason for the separation is not entirely clear; apparently she felt that Seymour had abandoned the "second work of faith" message, and she also objected to Seymour's marriage to Jennie Moore on May 13, 1908, arguing that he should not marry due to the soon coming of the Lord. At any rate, when she and Clara Lum left the Azusa Street Mission, they took with them the mailing list for *The Apostolic Faith* and published the paper from her mission in Portland.

In the summer of 1907, Crawford held a camp meeting in Portland that drew crowds of a thousand people, and reportedly one hundred received the Holy Ghost. (A later report lowered the number to less than one hundred.) Although her loose organization of missions never had more than five thousand followers, its influence reached a much larger number through its publications. In the months after she began publishing *The Apostolic Faith* in Portland, its circulation reached eighty thousand, about twice as many as when it was published at the Azusa Street Mission.

The May 1908 issue of *The Apostolic Faith* was the last published from the Azusa Street Mission. Crawford had an article in this issue, and Seymour had three, but it is clear that Crawford was in control of the issue. In the masthead, she informed readers of the paper's address change to Portland: "For the next issues of this paper address The Apostolic Faith Campmeeting, Portland, Ore."

In the summer of 1908, Crawford again held a camp meeting near Portland. It was at this camp meeting that a Canadian Baptist pastor, Frank J. Ewart, received the Holy Ghost. Ewart later became a prominent Pentecostal leader in Los Angeles, as well as an important leader in the Oneness Pentecostal movement.

William H. Durham

One of the most influential ministers who visited the Azusa Street Mission to receive the Holy Ghost was William Durham, pastor of a Holiness mission on North Avenue in Chicago. Born in Kentucky in 1873, Durham joined the Baptist church when he was eighteen years of age, but in his testimony on March 19, 1907, printed in the February/March 1907 issue of *The Apostolic Faith*,

William Durham on left

he wrote that he was converted nine years earlier. Shortly after his conversion, he embraced the Holiness doctrine of sanctification and entered into the ministry. He became the pastor of Chicago's North Avenue Mission in 1901.

Durham was popular as a Holiness preacher, traveling "as an evangelist from coast to coast, and preached the gospel in almost every large city in the United States, speaking to as high as 1,000 people at a time, often seeing from twenty-five to one hundred at the altar in a single service." But neither his experience nor his successful ministry satisfied him.

Durham heard of the Pentecostal outpouring at the Azusa Street Mission from John C. Sinclair, a minister and pastor who had been ordained by John Alexander Dowie. On November 19, 1906, during the time of Parham's revival in Zion, Sinclair received the Holy Ghost and his church became the first Pentecostal mission in Chicago. After visiting Sinclair's mission, Durham was convinced that the work was of God and began seeking the baptism of the Holy Ghost.

Durham felt that the Lord impressed him to go to Los Angeles and to seek the Spirit baptism. He arrived in Los Angeles on February 8, 1907, and attended his first service at the Azusa Street Mission two days later. On March 2, 1907, he received the Holy Ghost. On his way back to Chicago, he preached in Colorado Springs, Colorado, where about fifty people came to the altar and several received the Holy Ghost. He then preached for two weeks in Denver and twice in Des Moines, Iowa, before returning to Chicago on March 16. He reported that on the next Sunday the attendance at the North Avenue Mission was the largest in its history and "the altar was so full, that it was hard to deal with the people."

Durham's ministry soon made his North Avenue Mission a Pentecostal revival center known across North

America and even in foreign nations. He published a magazine, *Pentecostal Testimony*, which had a wide circulation in North America and worldwide. The rapid growth of the North Avenue Mission soon spawned other missions in the city, some along ethnic lines. By May 1908, there were thirteen or fourteen Pentecostal missions in Chicago, many of which were associated with Durham.

Hundreds, perhaps thousands, of people received the Holy Ghost under Durham's ministry from the spring of 1907 until his death in the summer of 1912. Early in his Pentecostal ministry, he wrote, "The Spirit falls like rain wherever I preach His word, and it seems there is no effort on my part." Frank Ewart wrote that Durham's pulpit ministry drew thousands of people everywhere and that his anointed preaching would bring a deep conviction and realization of God's presence.

Durham's leadership was influential in bringing many future Pentecostal leaders into the Pentecostal experience, including E. N. Bell, A. H. Argue, and William H. Piper. For a while, Robert and Aimee Semple assisted Durham in the North Avenue Mission before they left for mission work in Hong Kong. Andrew D. Urshan and his Persian group attended Durham's mission for a short while in 1910 before establishing a mission of their own.

CHAPTER TEN

THE FINISHED WORK ISSUE

William Durham was more than a gifted preacher; he was also known as a theologian unequaled in the Pentecostal movement. He became particularly known for introducing the doctrine he called "The Finished Work of Calvary," which he began proclaiming as early as 1908. This doctrinal position denied the Holiness movement's teaching that sanctification was a second definite work of grace subsequent to salvation.

Durham believed that God did not need two experiences to cleanse a person from sin, but that when God saves a person He also sanctifies him at that moment and then continues to sanctify him as he grows spiritually. Durham rejected the Holiness teaching that salvation cleansed only the outward man, leaving the inward man still carnal and sinful. He argued, "Salvation is an inward work. It means a change of heart. It means a change of nature. It means old things pass away and all things become new. It means that all condemnation and guilt is removed. It means that the old man, or old nature, which was sinful and depraved and which was the very thing in us that was condemned, is crucified with Christ." In other words, a person is not saved if his heart is still evil and his nature remains carnal.

Durham sincerely believed that the teaching of sanctification as a second work of grace was not biblical; moreover, he observed that people received the Holy Ghost without experiencing a second work of sanctification. He appealed for a return to the same gospel preached in the Book of Acts by the apostles, who did not teach or practice a second work of sanctification subsequent to salvation.

At a large Pentecostal convention in Chicago in 1910, Durham preached his Finished Work message, which found both acceptance and rejection by Pentecostals. Most of the opposition came from the churches located in the Southeast that had organized along the Holiness doctrine and from the Apostolic Faith groups led by Parham, Seymour, and Crawford. In the next two years, however, most Pentecostals in North America who did not belong to an organization accepted his Finished Work doctrine. The doctrinal dispute between the Second Work and Finished Work groups was not reconciled, resulting in the first major division in the Pentecostal movement, a division that still exists today.

In the spring of 1910, Howard Goss preached a three-week meeting for Durham in Chicago and became convinced of the Finished Work message. He then invited Durham to preach the Finished Work message during the summer camp meeting in Malvern, Arkansas. After this camp meeting, most ministers in the Midwest, Texas, Mississippi, Tennessee, and Alabama who looked to Howard

The Upper Room Mission in Los Angeles

Goss, E. N. Bell, H. G. Rodgers, and M. M. Pinson for leadership accepted the Finished Work doctrinal position.

Durham's Ministry in Los Angeles

In February 1911, Durham took his Finished Work message to Los Angeles; however, Elmer K. Fisher, the pastor of the Upper Room Mission, would not permit him to preach his message in this large Pentecostal mission. Although Seymour was on a tour in the East, Durham was allowed to hold services in the Azusa Street Mission, which now had only a small black congregation.

Durham's powerful preaching in the Azusa Street Mission revived the glory of the earlier revival, drawing crowds from the other Pentecostal missions that overflowed the building. Bartleman wrote, "On Sunday the place was crowded and five hundred were turned away. The people would not leave their seats between meetings for fear of losing them." Indeed, so many Pentecostals from the other missions came to hear Durham that most Pentecostal missions in the area were left empty, including Fisher's Upper Room Mission, which closed during the meetings.

When Seymour returned to Los Angeles, he rejected Durham's message and closed the Azusa Street Mission to him. Durham, forced to move, rented a large building at the corner of Seventh and Los Angeles Streets for the services, and the Sunday evening services had an attendance of about one thousand, and on weeknights about four hundred.

Durham's ministry in Los Angeles resulted not only in scores of people receiving the Holy Ghost but also in the Finished Work message being established. Most Pentecostals on the West Coast accepted Durham's message, including such leaders as Frank Bartleman, Glenn Cook, R. J. Scott, R. E. McAlister, and Frank Ewart. Durham appointed Ewart, who had recently moved from Canada to Los Angeles, to be the assistant pastor of his large congregation in the city.

The following summer, while he was in Chicago, Durham became seriously ill with pneumonia. When he realized that he was dying, he requested to return to his home in Los Angeles. Although weak and dying, he arrived in Los Angeles on Friday, July 5, 1912, and died on Sunday morning, July 7. The funeral service was conducted in the mission on the corner of Seventh and Los Angeles Streets with an attendance of at least one thousand. He was buried in the Inglewood Cemetery in Los Angeles.

Although Durham's Pentecostal ministry lasted only five years and a few months due to his early death at the age of thirty-nine, he attained worldwide leadership and left a lasting doctrinal imprint upon the Pentecostal movement. In 1914, the Assemblies of God was organized along the Finished Work position. Almost all Oneness organizations are in the Finished Work group, and it is possible, if not probable, that Durham's appeal to the authority of the Bible and to the example of the apostolic church in the Book of Acts prepared the way for Oneness Pentecostals to discover, identify with, and proclaim the apostolic doctrine of salvation.

The First Theological Division: The Finished Work Doctrine

Durham's successful ministry in Los Angeles during the early months of 1911 convinced most Pentecostals on the West Coast of his Finished Work message, adding them to those who had already embraced this position in the Midwest, East, and South. When the Holiness Pentecostal organizations rejected the Finished Work doctrine, the Pentecostal movement was divided into two groups: the Holiness Pentecostal group, which taught a threefold experience—salvation by faith, sanctification as a second work of grace to destroy the sinful nature, and the baptism of the Holy Ghost—and the Finished Work group, which embraced a twofold experience—salvation by faith followed by the baptism of the Holy Ghost.

The Holiness Pentecostals included Parham's group, Seymour's group, Crawford's group, and former Holiness organizations located in the southeastern United States. The Holiness Pentecostal group consisted of about 40 percent of all Pentecostals, the Finished Work group about 60 percent.

CHAPTER ELEVEN

EARLY PENTECOSTAL LEADERS

By the end of 1909, the Azusa Street revival was over, but the sparks of the revival continued to ignite revivals around the world. We have already traced the spread of the revival from Los Angeles to areas along the West Coast, into the Midwestern states of Illinois, Indiana, Ohio, and into the Southeastern states of North and South Carolina, Georgia, Florida, Alabama, Tennessee, and Mississippi. We have also mentioned that many workers left the Azusa Street Mission to take the revival to foreign nations, including those in Africa, Asia, and Europe.

In this chapter we will briefly trace the ministries of Thomas B. Barratt, Frank Bartleman, L. C. Hall, and Frank Ewart.

Thomas Ball Barratt

Thomas B. Barratt was born in England in 1862, but in 1867 his family moved to Norway. In 1891 he was ordained as an elder in the Methodist Episcopal Church and then pastored churches in Norway. In 1906 he came to the United States hoping to raise funds to expand the structure of the Methodist Christian Mission he had founded in Oslo. Though his fund-raising efforts failed, the trip proved to be a turning point in his life and ministry. While staying at the Christian Alliance Missionary Home in New York, he learned about the Azusa Street revival from reading a copy of the first issue of *The Apostolic Faith*.

Although Barratt did not make a journey to Los Angeles, he wrote to the Azusa Street Mission asking for information and spiritual advice. He soon received a response from I. May Throop, a worker at the Azusa Street Mission. In her letter dated September 28, 1906, she encouraged him to surrender everything, "leaving all for Jesus, loosing of all but God," and closed with a prayer for his soon reception of the Holy Ghost.

Ten days later on October 8, Glenn Cook, who was serving as the managing editor of *The Apostolic Faith*, wrote to Barratt to encourage him in his seeking for the baptism of the Holy Ghost. Cook also wrote two other letters to Barratt. In one letter dated October 15, 1906, Cook first responded to a letter from Barratt, in which he stated that he had received the Holy Ghost but had not spoken in tongues. Cook did not dispute Barratt's experience; instead, he encouraged him to continue seeking until he received the sign of speaking in tongues, for "speaking in tongues should follow the baptism . . . as a sign to you of Pentecost." About two weeks later, Cook wrote a third letter again exhorting Barratt to allow God to baptize him completely with the Holy Ghost: "You must keep your eyes on Jesus and doubt not that God has begun a work that he is able and willing to finish."

On November 15, 1906, Barratt received the gift of the Holy Ghost while attending a meeting with some Pentecostals who were en route from Azusa Street to take the Pentecostal experience to foreign nations. Barratt received the Holy Ghost when Maud Williams from Canada laid hands on him, but apparently he was not completely satisfied, for later the same night, after midnight, he asked a Brother and Sister Leatherman to lay hands on his head again.

Clara Lum, another worker at the Azusa Street Mission, wrote Barratt that, when she had read aloud his letter in a service at the Azusa Street Mission that told of his receiving the Holy Ghost, Gaston Cashwell, who had come to Azusa Street from North Carolina, was baptized with the Holy Ghost.

Upon his return to Norway in December 1906, Barratt immediately began spreading the Pentecostal experience not only in Norway but also in other European nations. In his meetings Barratt drew large crowds, often as large as 1,500 to 2,000 people. During 1907, he started fifty-one Pentecostal missions in Norway alone. By 1911, Barratt had held meetings in England, Finland, Estonia, and Russia, leaving Pentecostal converts and missions in these nations. His early Pentecostal ministry laid the foundation in Russia for later Pentecostal ministers such as Frank Bartleman and Andrew D. Urshan.

Frank Bartleman

Frank Bartleman was born on December 14, 1871, in Bucks County, Pennsylvania, and grew up on a farm. His father belonged to the Roman Catholic Church, and his mother came from a Quaker family; however, Frank was converted in the Baptist Temple in Philadelphia in 1893 and was licensed to preach by the Baptists. But Frank Bartleman was not one to stay very long in one location or with one church group. In 1897 he left the Baptist ministry to join the Salvation Army. In 1900 he married Miss Ladd and joined the Wesleyan Methodist church, and for a short time, he served as pastor in Corry, Pennsylvania. He then left Pennsylvania and moved to Denver, Colorado, where he worked with Alma White in her Pillar of Fire church. He then moved to Sacramento, California, and then in late 1904 he arrived in Los Angeles, where he became associated with the events before and during the outpouring of the Holy Ghost in that city.

During 1905 Bartleman ministered in Peniel missions and Holiness churches in the Los Angeles area. Late in

Frank Bartleman

1905 he joined Joseph Smale's New Testament Church in praying for an outpouring of the Holy Ghost, but at this time the sign of speaking in tongues was not known to them. Both Smale and Bartleman wrote letters to Evan Roberts, the leader of the famous Welsh Revival in England, asking for advice and prayers for a similar revival in America.

In March and early April 1906 Bartleman attended a few of William Seymour's prayer meetings, first in the Lee home and later in the Asberry home on Bonnie Brae Street. Although Bartleman was not present when the Holy Ghost was first poured out upon Seymour's group on April 9, he was present at the Bonnie Brae house on April 15, and he attended some of the first services at the Azusa Street Mission.

As early as anyone else, Bartleman realized the importance of the outpouring of the Spirit in Los Angeles at the Azusa Street Mission. Although the two-story forty-by-sixty-foot building was old and crude, with a dirt lower floor and unfinished walls, he watched the small group gradually grow until he could write in August 1906 that revival had come to Los Angeles. More than any other person, Bartleman traced the beginnings, captured the dynamic, unfolded the drama, described the scenes, chronicled the happenings, and preserved the story of the revival that transformed Pentecostalism into a worldwide movement.

Beginning in 1906, Bartleman used his gifted writing skills to write articles about the Azusa Street revival for publications in Holiness periodicals in North America, especially in the Midwest and South. During the three years of the revival, more than five hundred of his articles were published in Holiness periodicals, many of which were reprinted after they appeared in one periodical. Some of his articles appeared in periodicals in England. After reading the articles, some Holiness ministers made the trip to Los Angeles to receive the Holy Ghost, and many others were stirred to seek the baptism of the Spirit at home.

In the summer of 1906, Bartleman opened a mission on the corner of Eighth Street and Maple Avenue, and it was here that he received the Holy Ghost on August 16. In late September or early October, Bartleman turned over the building and mission to William H. Pendleton, a Holiness pastor who with his congregation of thirty-five people had been turned out of the Holiness church and evicted from their church building when they received the Holy Ghost.

As the revival spread across North America, Bartleman, like some at the Azusa Street Mission, embarked with his family on a preaching tour to the Midwest and East beginning in March 1907. He preached in Denver, Colorado; Chicago, Illinois; several cities in Ohio, New York, Maine, Pennsylvania, North Carolina, and South Carolina; St. Louis, Missouri; Topeka, Kansas; and Colorado Springs, Colorado. He arrived back in Los Angeles on December 5, 1907.

He made a second preaching tour of the United States that lasted eleven months, beginning on March 25, 1908, and ending with his return to Los Angeles on February 26, 1909. Although he preached in some of the same places he had visited in 1907, this tour was primarily to other states, cities, and churches. Three months later in May 1909, he made a month-long trip to preach in Hawaii.

It is remarkable that Bartleman, who was always in poverty and at the point of hunger, made any of these tours. However, it is even more remarkable that he made a round-the-world tour beginning on March 17, 1910, and returning to Los Angeles on February 25, 1911.

But his travels were not finished, for in the fall of 1912 he embarked with his family to Europe, where he lived and ministered for about two years in England, Germany, Sweden, Finland, and Russia. He was probably the first American Pentecostal minister to preach to the Russian people in Russia, predating Andrew Urshan's ministry in St. Petersburg in 1916 and the missionary work of Ivan E. Voranaev, an Assemblies of God missionary who arrived in the southern part of Russia in about 1921.

Of interest to Oneness Pentecostals is that Bartleman accepted both the Finished Work doctrine and the message of baptism in Jesus' name.

Lemuel Charles Hall

L. C. Hall was born on September 16, 1867, in Potosi, Missouri, and grew up in a prominent Southern family. His father was a noted physician from a long line of physicians. His mother's father had served as governor of Alabama, United States senator, and Minister Plenipotentiary to Russia. When Hall was nineteen years old, he was selected to be a cadet in West Point Military Academy and was admitted on September 1, 1887. However, he soon decided against a military career and resigned from the academy on December 1, 1887.

In 1892 he enrolled in Washington University Law School in St. Louis, Missouri. But his interest in being an attorney lasted only a few months. Although he had not attended church services for several years, one evening on his way home from the university he was troubled about his sinfulness and prayed to God to save him. When he arrived at his home he shut himself in his room and continued to pray until he had dedicated his life to God and felt His approval.

L. C. Hall

On the following Sunday, he attended a Methodist church, where he heard Dr. H. C. Morrison, a notable minister and the president of the new Asbury College. Hall immediately sold his law books and enrolled in Asbury College. In 1893 he transferred to Vanderbilt University in Nashville, Tennessee, where he remained a student in 1894, 1895, and 1896. During his first year at Vanderbilt, he married Mary McGee, and on April 8, 1893, he was ordained a minister in the Southern Methodist Episcopal Church.

After his university studies, L. C. Hall returned with his wife to St. Louis and began an independent church. However, they soon heard of John Alexander Dowie and were so impressed with his writing that a few years later they visited Zion, became members of the movement, and were ordained into its ministry. Hall and his wife lived for a short time in Chicago before moving to San Antonio, where he served as pastor in the Zion church there. Then a few years later, tragedy came to his life when his wife died.

While Hall was pastoring in San Antonio, D. C. O. Opperman, who had been living in Zion, Illinois, visited him in 1905 and 1906. During this time Opperman accepted the Apostolic Faith message preached by Charles Parham and was seeking the baptism of the Holy Ghost. In February 1907, the Apostolic Faith workers in Texas held a short-term Bible school in Waco, Texas. After the school was over in March, a group led by A. G. Canada held a revival in San Antonio. With the group were Opperman and his wife and T. Matthew Bowen, who later pastored a Oneness church in Houston for many years.

During the revival services in San Antonio, Hall received the gift of the Holy Ghost. His leadership talent and skill, along with his anointed preaching, almost immediately elevated him to a place of leadership among

Pentecostals. He was highly respected and esteemed and became a favorite camp meeting and conference speaker throughout the Midwest. He was also among the first in the Midwest to accept the Oneness message and to be rebaptized in the name of Jesus Christ. His widespread influence persuaded hundreds of others to follow him into the Jesus Name movement. In 1910, Hall married Jean Campbell, who in 1906 had moved from Zion, Illinois, with Marie Burgess to pioneer a church in New York City.

After the Oneness people were forced out of the Assemblies of God in 1916, Hall was among the 154 ministers who met in Eureka Springs, Arkansas, from December 28, 1916, to January 3, 1917, to form the first Oneness organization, the General Assembly of the Apostolic Assemblies. Early the following year, in January 1918, when the Apostolic Assembly of the Apostolic Assemblies merged with the Pentecostal Assemblies of the World, Hall and his wife became licensed ministers with the new organization, and Hall was chosen to serve on the Credential Committee. At the General Assembly held in October 1919, Hall was chosen to serve on the Resolution Committee. He was also chosen to be a member of the Board of General Elders.

After the division in the Pentecostal Assemblies of the World occurred in 1925, a group of ministers met in Jackson, Tennessee, to form a Oneness organization, which they named The Pentecostal Ministerial Alliance. Hall was elected to be its first chairman.

Frank J. Ewart

Born in Bendigo, Victoria, Australia, in 1876, Frank Ewart began his ministry as a bush missionary in the

Baptist church. In 1903 his health broke, and in June 1903 he immigrated to Canada, where he had relatives. He first went to Weyburn, Saskatchewan, to be near a cousin who lived on a farm. The Canadian Baptist organization in Winnipeg, Manitoba, accepted his ministerial credentials, ordained him, and helped him secure a pastorate. During this time he married and for a few years served as pastor of two churches.

Sometime in the early months of 1908, he received a letter from his brother-in-law inviting Ewart and his wife to visit him at his farm near New Westminster, British Columbia. In the letter his brother-in-law told of a religious movement that had "invaded" the area in a church in which the pastor and every member claimed to have received the gift of the Holy Ghost with the sign of speaking in other tongues, exactly as the apostles and early church experienced. He also wrote of people claiming to be healed. Ewart, whose health had turned worse, took a furlough from his church, and he and his wife went to New Westminster.

During the few services at the "invaded" church they attended in New Westminster, they heard about a large camp meeting being held in Portland, Oregon, and they decided to attend. At the campground they felt the power of God's Spirit, and the Ewarts began praying earnestly for the baptism of the Holy Ghost. At midnight on the twenty-first day that Ewart had been praying, he received "a mighty infilling with the Holy Ghost," speaking in tongues as the Spirit gave the utterance. He had also asked God for physical healing, which happened when he was filled with the Holy Ghost, and his vision was so corrected that he did not need the glasses he had worn for years.

When they returned to their church in Canada, the church rejected his testimony of receiving the Holy Ghost and refused to let him continue his pastoral ministry. Moreover, the Baptist Church board summoned him to question him about his experience. The board tried to get him to discredit or compromise his experience, but when he refused, they dismissed him from their ministry.

Three years later, in January or February 1911, Ewart moved to Los Angeles. He had only recently arrived in the city when William Durham came to Los Angeles on February 25, 1911, to bring the Finished Work message to the West Coast. Being from a Baptist background, Ewart had no trouble accepting Durham's teaching. He then worked with Durham during several months of revival meetings.

When Durham returned to Chicago later in 1911, he appointed Ewart to serve as assistant pastor of the large Los Angeles assembly while he was gone. The following year Durham became fatally ill while he was in Chicago, but he was determined to go to Los Angeles before his death. Durham arrived in Los Angeles on July 5, 1912, and two days later, on Sunday, July 7, he died.

As Durham had directed, Ewart assumed the pastorate of the large congregation and served in this position for another year, until after the Worldwide Apostolic Faith Camp Meeting in 1913. After this camp meeting, Ewart opened another mission in Los Angeles, with R. E. McAlister and Glenn Cook as his assistants. However, several months later Ewart accepted the invitation of Warren Fisher, pastor of Victoria Hall on Spring Street, to join his congregation with Victoria Hall.

---------CHAPTER TWELVE---------

THE NEW ISSUE

The second doctrinal issue that divided Pentecostals—the first was the Finished Work issue—was known as the "New Issue" and began over the formula used in water baptism. This issue was ignited at the Worldwide Apostolic Faith Camp Meeting held in Los Angeles in April 1913. This large Pentecostal camp meeting was intended to promote unity in the Pentecostal movement, which now had churches in most states and provinces in North America and in many foreign nations. R. J. Scott, a Canadian who had been a worker at the Azusa Street Mission, was the chairman of the camp meeting committee, and Mary Woodworth-Etter was the featured camp evangelist. Pentecostal ministers and laity from nearly every state and province in North America and missionaries from many foreign fields could be counted among the multitude in attendance.

From the beginning, the camp meeting was a success. The large tent for the services overflowed with people, many were healed of various diseases, and about five hundred people were "saved and baptized in the Spirit." A large number of ministers filled not only the platform but also rows of seats in the tent, and several preachers were invited to speak during the day services.

Toward the end of the camp meeting, the camp meeting chairman, R. J. Scott, asked R. E. McAlister to preach the baptismal service for those wanting to be baptized. In his sermon McAlister pointed out that the early church in the Book of Acts did not use the trinitarian formula but consistently baptized in the name of Jesus Christ or the Lord Jesus.

Evidently, McAlister did not intend to condemn the use of the trinitarian formula or to suggest that Pentecostals must or should use the apostolic formula in water baptism. After a preacher stopped him and took him aside on the platform to warn him not to preach that doctrine, McAlister returned to the pulpit and explained that, although what he had preached about baptism in the name of Jesus Christ was scripturally correct, he did not mean to imply that it was wrong to use the traditional trinitarian formula; he only intended to point out the formula used by the apostles and early church in Acts.

Although McAlister may have unwittingly opened the issue of apostolic water baptism, his scriptural exposition could not be ignored by those wanting to return to the apostolic faith. The matter would not leave the thoughts of many of the preachers. They asked, "Why did the apostolic church consistently use the name of Jesus in water baptism and never once used the words of Matthew 28:19?" Several ministers spent time discussing this topic, and some began praying for a scriptural answer.

After the camp meeting, Ewart invited McAlister to

his home in Los Angeles and asked McAlister to explain his understanding of why the apostles and early church baptized in the name of Jesus Christ and did not repeat the words in Matthew 28:19. McAlister explained that *Lord Jesus Christ* was the singular "name" in Matthew 28:19 and related to the terms Father, Son, and Holy Ghost. For the next several months, Ewart and McAlister worked together in Los Angeles with Glenn Cook and G. T. Haywood, and the subject of Jesus Name baptism was often discussed. Ewart stated that, when McAlister left to return to his home in Canada, he had stressed that he did not want the issue of baptism to divide the Pentecostal movement. That same desire for unity was also in the heart of Ewart, Cook, Haywood, and most Pentecostals, but the desire to follow the scriptural pattern given in the Book of Acts and supported throughout the New Testament could not be ignored.

Eventually, Ewart found the answer to his question in Colossians 2:9. He later wrote, "I saw that as all the fullness of the Godhead dwelt in Jesus, bodily; therefore baptism, as the Apostles administered it, in the Name of the Lord Jesus Christ, was the one and only fulfillment of Matthew 28:19." Having embraced the absolute deity of Jesus and Jesus Name baptism after a year of study and prayer, Ewart wrote that he gathered a group of workers and "rented and pitched a tent on the east side of the city of Los Angeles, and began to proclaim my new revelation."

On April 15, 1914, Ewart baptized Glenn Cook in the name of Jesus Christ and Cook in turn baptized Ewart in the name of Jesus Christ. This one event marked the beginning of the Jesus Name movement in this century.

—————CHAPTER THIRTEEN—————

EARLY ORGANIZATIONAL EFFORTS

By the summer of 1906, Charles Parham's Apostolic Faith movement had taken root not only in Kansas, Oklahoma, and Missouri, but had also rapidly spread across Texas and had been established in California. During the next year, it would also take root in Illinois, Indiana, Oregon, Tennessee, North Carolina, South Carolina, Georgia, New York, Ohio, Florida, Alabama, Arkansas, Iowa, and in several other foreign countries, including Canada, England, Norway, Sweden, Finland, India, Liberia, and Germany.

During the early years of the Pentecostal revival, Charles Parham stated that his intention for the Apostolic Faith movement was not to form another church denomination or organization but to restore the experience of the baptism of the Holy Ghost to Christianity. He felt that if he were to organize the movement it would become a denomination and would be in danger of becoming as worldly and spiritually barren as much of modern Christendom. Thus he saw the Pentecostal revival as a restoration of apostolic experience and truth among Christians in general.

However, with the phenomenal growth of the Apostolic Faith movement from 1903 to 1906, Parham apparently recognized that some form of organizational structure was needed to oversee and guide the eight to thirteen thousand people who had come into the movement. In April 1906 Parham began issuing ministerial credentials to his workers in the name of the Apostolic Faith movement. In August 1906 he formed the first organizational structure when he appointed W. F. Carothers, the pastor of the Apostolic Faith church in Brunner, Texas, to the position of general field director and Howard Goss as director of the movement's ministers and missions in Texas. For himself, Parham took the title of projector of the Apostolic Faith movement. When William Seymour, who had by this time opened the Azusa Street Mission, learned that Parham was issuing ministerial credentials, he wrote to Carothers requesting a license, which was granted to him.

In January 1907, however, Parham decided to resign his position and published his resignation in the January 1907 issue of *The Apostolic Faith*. In his published resignation, he denied ever having any intention of organizing the movement and that the structure he had formed was meant to be temporary. He wrote, "In resigning my position as Projector of the Apostolic Faith Movement, I simply followed a well considered plan of mine, made many years ago, never to receive honor of men, or to establish a new church. I was called a pope, a Dowie, etc., and everywhere looked upon as a leader or a would-be leader and proselyter. These designations have always been an abomination to me and since God has given almost universal light to the world on Pentecost there is no further need of my holding the official leadership of the Apostolic Faith Movement." He called upon his followers to "cease wasting time at this juncture in systematizing or organizing the work of God."

Parham's resignation, however, was not the event that destroyed Parham's leadership role and influence; rather it was being arrested on July 19, 1907, in San Antonio and being charged with the "commission of an unnatural offense," i.e., sodomy. Both Parham and the man alleged to have committed the offense with him were committed to jail. Although the charges against Parham were eventually dropped, the local newspaper, *The San Antonio Light*, had reported the incident, and the news of Parham's arrest quickly spread throughout the movement, causing concern, confusion, and chaos among his followers. Whether Parham was guilty or not may never be conclusively known, but the effects of the arrest destroyed Parham's influence among most of his followers. Howard Goss had resigned his position as the director of the Apostolic Faith movement in Texas in May of 1907, and Parham's legal trouble temporarily left the sixty-five ministerial workers in Texas without any organized leadership. However, they soon formed a loose fellowship in the state under Goss, L. C. Hall, D. C. O. Opperman, and A. G. Canada. Unfortunately—and not surprisingly—critics of the Apostolic Faith movement seized upon Parham's arrest as an opportunity to discredit the movement.

In late 1906 Parham and Seymour clashed during Parham's visit to the Azusa Street Mission, and soon afterward Seymour separated his mission from Parham. In early 1907 Seymour organized the Pacific Apostolic Faith movement with a ministerial board of leaders at the mission, which examined ministerial applications and issued ministerial credentials. After the Azusa Street revival faded in 1909, this organization mainly served only the small congregation that remained at the Azusa Street Mission.

Florence Louise Crawford, who left the Azusa Street Mission in December 1906, founded the Apostolic Faith Mission in Portland, Oregon, in 1907. This Apostolic Faith organization grew to about five thousand followers before Crawford's death in 1936. Today it continues under the same name with headquarters in Portland.

In the southeastern United States, under the preaching of G. B. Cashwell, the Pentecostal message was accepted by several Holiness church organizations, including the Church of God, the Pentecostal Holiness Church, the Fire-Baptized Holiness Church, and the Free Will Baptist Church. Basically these church organizations were patterned along the lines of the Methodist church, and for the most part, they have continued with their organized structures since their acceptance of the Pentecostal experience.

The majority of unorganized Pentecostals resided in the Midwest and West. For the most part, they had accepted the Finished Work message taught by William Durham and had rejected Parham's leadership after his arrest in 1907. Although these former followers of Parham still used the name Apostolic Faith movement, they soon began referring to themselves as Pentecostals to distance themselves from Parham and his remaining followers. These Pentecostals in Texas, Arkansas,

Oklahoma, and other states were held together under the leadership of prominent ministers such as Howard A. Goss, D. C. O. Opperman, L. C. Hall, A. G. Canada, A. P. Collins, and E. N. Bell. These leaders conducted camp meetings, conferences, training seminars, and revivals in order to bring the people together for fellowship, unity, and teaching. In 1909 they also published *The Apostolic Faith*, edited by Goss and published in Fort Worth, Texas. When Goss turned over the pastorate of the church in Malvern, Arkansas, to Bell, he also turned over the editorship of *The Apostolic Faith* to him.

This loose fellowship could not adequately keep unity or preserve scriptural teaching and practices. Most leaders knew of self-proclaimed Pentecostal preachers who were unethical in conduct and unscriptural in doctrine. These preachers peddled their false teachings and preyed on congregations whenever and wherever they found opportunity. Goss wrote about preachers who were proclaiming wild "revelations" that brought confusion, disunity, and chaos among the churches. He reasoned that a stronger form of organization would help retain unity in doctrine and purity in fellowship. Goss said that the first steps taken to strengthen the organization occurred when "it was unanimously agreed at one of our conferences that every minister who received a new revelation was not to preach or teach it publicly until the next conference. Then he was to subject it to his brethren in open session. If none of his hearers could tear it to pieces scripturally, nor 'shoot it full of holes,' and if it came through still in one piece, all preachers would be at liberty to preach it, if they wished."

It addition to the four associations using the name

Apostolic Faith (Parham's original group, Seymour's group in Los Angeles, Florence Crawford's group in Portland, and the former followers of Parham in the Midwest under the leadership of Goss, Bell, Opperman, Hall, and others), Pentecostal associations were also being formed in other areas and states. Among these were former followers of John Alexander Dowie, who had become Pentecostal, former churches and ministers of A. B. Simpson's Christian and Ministerial Alliance who converted to Pentecostalism, the Elim ministry in the Northeast, ministers in Canada, and ministers in the West.

One fellowship that was to become important to the history of the Assemblies of God and consequently of the United Pentecostal Church International was formed in the Southeast, particularly in Alabama and Mississippi, but also extended into other states. By 1909 H. G. Rodgers, M. M. Pinson, and J. W. Ledbetter had established several Pentecostal churches in Alabama and Mississippi and had formed an association among them. In 1909 at a conference at Dothan, Alabama, they adopted the name of Church of God and prepared to license and ordain ministers and apply for recognition from the Southern Clergy Bureau for reduced railroad fares. Rodgers was elected as chairman of the organization, and Ledbetter was elected as secretary. However, since the chosen name was already used by other church groups, confusion delayed their progress. When they decided to change the name to Church of God in Christ, they discovered that this name was already being used by C. H. Mason's predominantly black organization in Memphis.

A few Pentecostal ministers sought credentials from one of the Apostolic Faith associations, while others obtained credentials from faith homes and rescue missions. It became a matter for individual ministers. Most Pentecostal ministers were not concerned about ministerial credentials, and some resisted even the appearance of belonging to any organized religious group. Most, however, saw value in having a ministerial license, even if only to receive discounted train fares.

Perhaps as early as 1907, Howard Goss obtained ministerial credentials from Mason's organization. Later in 1910, probably after discussing the matter with Rodgers and Pinson, Goss made an arrangement with Mason to issue ministerial credentials to white ministers in the Apostolic Faith movement and to those in Rodgers's association. This was not a merger; Goss wrote that this arrangement was primarily for business purposes. Since Mason had incorporated the Church of God in Christ, this arrangement allowed white ministers in both Goss's and Rodgers's groups to be eligible to receive clergy railroad discounts, as well as other civil recognition. Goss issued credentials to white ministers in the name Church of God in Christ, but they were issued separately from Mason's group. Some of Goss's group continued to call themselves Apostolic Faith, but most of them soon preferred the name Church of God in Christ.

The matters of a church name and ministerial credentials led to a discussion of a merger between the association led by Rodgers and Pinson and the group led by Goss and Bell. In 1911 Pinson, the editor of *Word and Witness*, and Bell, the editor of *The Apostolic Faith*, decided to merge these publications of the two segments of the white Church of God in Christ, with *The Apostolic Faith* being absorbed into *Word and Witness* and Bell assuming the editorial responsibilities. In 1912 Bell announced a camp meeting for the "Churches of God in Christ of the Apostolic Faith people." This camp meeting was held in Eureka Springs, Arkansas, and was attended by more than three hundred people and set the stage for the consummation of the merger of the two segments in June 1913 at a convention held in Meridian, Mississippi. A ministerial list issued at that meeting contained 352 names from both segments.

Although this merger created a loose association of a large body of ministers, it became apparent that a more structured organization was needed to preserve the Pentecostal work. Goss wrote, "As our numbers increased, the influx brought with it leaders who did not believe in organization at all; some even preached that anything of that nature (when committed to paper) was of the devil. Opposing this viewpoint was the definite system existing in the New Testament under the Apostles." He noted that some leaders were operating "unwritten organizations" by gathering churches and ministers who were like-minded in doctrine and standards. He commented that these "unwritten organizations" often divided the people into small and competing groups. He wrote, "The cohesiveness which God had given us in the baptism of the Holy Ghost through love was rapidly being lost through a lack of cooperation, and the spirit then abroad in the land was endeavoring to separate us."

Goss, with his desire to form a better organization than the loose association of the white segment of Church of God in Christ, enlisted Bell to work on a solution to better organize the movement. Later they discovered that Opperman also shared their concerns. Goss wrote, "Of necessity we secretly discussed calling a conference to organize the work. So in November of 1913, Brother Bell and I ventured to announce a conference at Hot Springs, Arkansas, from April 2 to April 12, 1914. We signed the original call ourselves." This call appeared in the December 20, 1913, issue of the *Word and Witness*. It was a formal call for a "General Convention of Pentecostal Saints and Churches of God in Christ," and was signed by M. M. Pinson, A. P. Collins, H. A. Goss, D. C. O. Opperman, and E. N. Bell. This convention would establish an organization called the Assemblies of God, from which the Oneness Jesus Name movement would emerge.

THE FORMATION OF THE ASSEMBLIES OF GOD

After Charles Parham's leadership was discredited in 1907, most of the people in the Apostolic Faith movement in the Midwest separated from him to form their own fellowship. Howard Goss, whom Parham appointed in 1906 to be the field director of the Apostolic Faith workers in the state of Texas, at first tried to keep the workers together. When this failed he resigned his position as field director, an act that separated him from Parham's leadership.

Although these former followers of Parham still used the name Apostolic Faith, they separated from Parham and began to refer to themselves as Pentecostals. At the camp meeting in the summer of 1907, A. G. Canada was appointed to be field director; in 1908 D. C. O. Opperman replaced Canada as field director. The leadership of prominent ministers such as Howard Goss, A. G. Canada, D. C. O. Opperman, L. C. Hall, A. P. Collins, and W. F. Carothers strengthened the movement. These leaders conducted camp meetings, conferences, training seminars, and revivals to bring people together for fellowship, unity, and teaching.

In the fall of 1907, Howard Goss and his wife, Millicent, with some workers, evangelized and established churches in several cities and communities in Texas, including McGregor, San Antonio, Austin, and Snyder. Their success in Austin, a city that had not heard the Pentecostal message, was tremendous. In tent meetings held on East Twelfth Street and East First Street, and then in a hall uptown, about two hundred people received the Holy Ghost and many people were healed. When they left the city, they turned over the congregation to J. D. Shumack.

In the winter of 1907, Goss and his wife went to Galena, Kansas, Goss's hometown, to preach a revival in the church. During the revival, Goss's mother received the gift of the Holy Ghost.

The Gosses returned to Texas in April 1908 in time to attend a two-day conference on April 20-21. They

Howard Goss

stayed in Texas through July, preaching in San Antonio, Austin, Houston, and San Marcos. In July they attended the camp meeting held in Houston at the Brunner campground and tabernacle, where they met E. J. Bayse, a Pentecostal businessman living in Stuttgart, Arkansas. Bayse purchased a large, new gospel tent for Goss and urged him to come to Arkansas to establish churches in this new field.

Although Goss continued to take an active role in the work in Texas by conducting camp meetings and revivals, attending conferences and training schools, and helping to establish more missions, for the next several years Arkansas became his home and headquarters for his ministerial and leadership activities. He held tent revivals and camps in many cities in Arkansas, Oklahoma, and Missouri, as well as in Kansas, Iowa, Illinois, Mississippi, and Louisiana, providing leadership and inspiration for the establishment of hundreds of churches in these states. Of course, he was not alone in this work; many other ministers and workers were also working with him in the spread of the Pentecostal experience throughout the Midwest and South.

In 1908 Goss and his wife held an extended revival in Lucas, Iowa, from January 23 until April 13 in order to open a mission in this town. At least nineteen people received the Holy Ghost, and Goss baptized fourteen in water. They also held meetings for two weeks in Centerville, Iowa.

Pentecostals in the Midwest continued to grow rapidly as missions and churches became established in hundreds of cities and towns, with thousands of new Pentecostals, both ministers and laymen, being added to the movement. By 1910 the Midwest contained the largest number of unorganized Pentecostals in North America.

Pentecostals in other areas of North America were also increasing in numbers, especially in the West and the Southeast. Many missions and churches had already been established in California, in areas such as Los Angeles, Oakland, Stockton, and San Diego. Although Florence Crawford had organized a group in Portland, Oregon, and William Seymour had started the Pacific Apostolic Faith movement in Los Angeles, most Pentecostal missions, ministers, and laypeople fellowshipped in a loose association of missions and ministers.

Late in1907 Howard Goss obtained ministerial credentials from the Church of God in Christ, a predominantly black church organization located in Memphis, Tennessee, and he also received permission from C. H. Mason, the founder and leader of the Church of God in Christ, to issue ministerial credentials to white ministers using the name Church of God in Christ. Later, Bell and a few other ministers received ministerial credentials through this arrangement.

At a convention held in Houston, beginning on January 1, 1909, D. C. O. Opperman was elected to be the field director of Texas. Goss was asked to be the editor of *The Apostolic Faith*. The convention was extended by a training school for ministers in Houston under the direction of Opperman. It was at this convention and school that Goss met E. N. Bell, and the two became close friends. A. P. Collins also attended this convention and school. The school ended on April 6, but Goss remained in Houston to work on *The Apostolic Faith* and to care for the churches in the Houston area. Goss worked on *The Apostolic Faith* from April 27 until it was ready for mailing on May 7. He finished mailing the 5,000 copies of *The Apostolic Faith* on May 13. On June 17 Goss left Houston for Arkansas to hold camp meetings in Stuttgart, Pine Bluff, Hot Springs, and Redfield.

On September 8, Howard and Millicent Goss began one of their most successful revival meetings in the town of Malvern, Arkansas. This revival lasted until December 26, with a total of 152 people receiving the Holy Ghost and Goss baptizing 110 people in water. This revival spirit continued into the next year with about 100 other people receiving the Holy Ghost. The converts were able to secure excellent property in Malvern, and they constructed a tabernacle for the winter months and later a church building for this new, but large, Pentecostal congregation.

It was perhaps during one of Bell's visits to this revival (Bell visited on October 12-15 and on December 6-7) that Goss asked him to assume the pastorate of the Malvern congregation. On January 8, 1910, Bell became the pastor. Goss then turned over the editorship of *The Apostolic Faith* to him. Later, in 1911, M. M. Pinson turned over the editorship of *Word and Witness* to Bell, and Bell absorbed *The Apostolic Faith* into *Word and Witness* and published the periodical under the name of *Word and Witness*.

On February 14, 1910, Howard and Millicent Goss left Malvern by train and arrived the same day in Chicago. In this city they preached at William Durham's mission many times, at William H. Piper's Stone Church several times, at John Sinclair's missions a few times, and two or three times at a small mission on Ashland Avenue. On March 4-6 Goss visited Zion, Illinois, and attended a service at Shiloh Tabernacle, as well as services at two Pentecostal missions in the city. They returned to Malvern by way of St. Louis, Missouri, where they ministered at S. D. Kinne's mission and at Harvey's Peoples Mission. They then spent three days in Memphis, where they preached at two missions. On April 20 Goss spent most of the day with Bell in Malvern, perhaps discussing Durham's Finished Work message.

During the business meeting at the Fort Worth camp meeting on July 10-24, Opperman was reelected as the field director in Texas. Goss related in his diary that he, Bell, and Opperman held a discussion on July 17, but he did not give the subject of the discussion. At the camp meeting held in Malvern on September 1-25, Durham preached his Finished Work message, which was well received by the ministers and laity.

Sometime in 1911 a proposal was probably discussed to merge the group led by Rodgers and Pinson with the group led by Opperman, Bell, and Goss. Rodgers called the merger a consolidation "with the Western work with Bro. Opperman," adopting the name of Church of God in Christ. This "consolidation" may have been approved at an elders' conference held during a camp meeting in Dallas. Goss chaired the conference on July 14, and the conference continued the next day. Another camp meeting was held in Eureka Springs, Arkansas, on July 16-30. In his diary Goss does not mention an elders' conference or convention held during this camp. However, he mentions an elders' conference during a convention held in late December 1911 in Houston. The elders' conference was held on December 28, and a general conference was held on December 29.

In early June 1912, Goss attended a convention in Nashville, Tennessee, probably sponsored by the group under Rodgers and Pinson. On July 10-22 a large camp meeting was held in Eureka Springs, perhaps the largest camp held in Arkansas. Goss noted in his diary that "about 400 visitors" attended the camp. Perhaps the large attendance was a result of the announcement in *Word and Witness* that the camp meeting was for the "Churches of God in Christ of the Apostolic Faith people."

It is interesting to note that another camp meeting was held in September 1912 in Hot Springs, Arkansas.

Pinson and his family attended this camp. Further, on October 12, Goss went to Malvern for a meeting with Bell and Pinson. Pinson chaired the meeting. We do not know the reason for this meeting, but it may have included plans for the June 1913 meeting in Meridian, Mississippi, at which the merger of the two groups was consummated. A ministerial list issued at this meeting contained 352 names from both groups, and an added note suggested that some names may have been missed.

Although this merger created only a loose association of a large body of ministers, it was a positive step toward dealing with disruptive ministers, wayward churches, and unscrupulous preachers. Still it became apparent to Goss that a more structured organization was needed to unify and preserve the Pentecostal work. Goss, with his desire for a stronger organization than the loose association of the white segment of Church of God in Christ, enlisted Bell to work on a solution to better organize the movement. They were encouraged when they learned that Opperman shared their concerns. Goss wrote, "Of necessity we secretly discussed calling a conference to organize the work. So in November of 1913, Brother Bell and I ventured to announce in *Word and Witness* a conference at Hot Springs, Arkansas, from April 2 to April 12, 1914. We signed the original call ourselves." This call appeared again in the December 20, 1913, issue of the *Word and Witness*. It was a formal call for a "General Convention of Pentecostal Saints and Churches of God in Christ," and was now signed by M. M. Pinson, A. P. Collins, Howard A. Goss, D. C. O. Opperman, and E. N. Bell. The signed statement of the formal call reads:

We desire at this time to make this preliminary announcement of this general meeting so that workers far and near, at home and abroad, may sidetrack everything else and be present. Laymen as well as preachers are invited. . . . This call is to all the churches of God in Christ, to all Pentecostal or Apostolic Faith Assemblies who desire with united purpose to co-operate in love and peace to push the interests of the kingdom of God everywhere. This is, however, only for saints who believe in the baptism with the Holy Ghost, with the signs following. Acts 2:4; 10:46; 19:6; Mark 16:16-18; I Cor. 12:8-11. Neither is this meeting for any captious, contrary, divisive, or contentious person. But we leave for the body itself to take up any subject it desires more than what is herein afterwards mentioned.

Five subjects to be considered at the meeting were listed. These subjects constitute the reasons for proposing an organization:

First—We come together that we may get a better understanding of what God would have us teach, that we may do away with so many divisions, both in doctrine and in the various names under which our Pentecostal people are working and incorporating. Let us come together as in Acts 15, to study the Word, and pray with and for each other—unity our chief aim.

Second—Again we come together that we may know how to conserve the work, that we may all build up and not tear down, both in home and foreign lands.

Third—We come together for another reason, that we may get a better understanding of the needs of each foreign field, and may know how to place our money in such a way that one mission or missionary shall not suffer, while another not any more worthy, lives in luxuries. Also that we may discourage wasting money on those who are running here and there accomplishing nothing, and may concentrate our support on those who mean business for our King.

Fourth—Many of the saints have felt the need of chartering the Churches of God in Christ, putting them on a legal basis, and thus obeying the laws of the land. . . .

Fifth—We may have a proposition to lay before the body for a general Bible Training School with a literary department for our people.

This announced proposal to organize the Pentecostal churches and people met a storm of opposition. Some people denounced it as unscriptural and warned of the danger of pride and church governmental authority over the work of the Spirit. But there were those who endorsed the proposal and joined in the appeal to organize. The appeal appeared two more times in the *Word and Witness*, each appeal with more explanation about the need to organize.

Goss, the pastor in Hot Springs, leased the Grand Opera House, located in the center of the resort town, for the convention, but he worried that only a small crowd would attend. He asked Opperman to come to Hot Springs in early spring to take charge of the preparations while he made an evangelistic tour of churches and camps, perhaps in an effort to encourage people to attend the convention. But his concerns were ill founded, for people came to the Hot Springs convention from many

Site of the founding of the Assemblies of God

areas of the nation and even from foreign lands. Twenty states were represented. More than 300 people attended with 128 registering as ministers and missionaries. The largest group came from the Midwest, especially from the merged white Churches of God in Christ led by Goss, Bell, Opperman, Collins, Rodgers, and Pinson. People from this association were predominant at the convention. Other leaders such as A. B. Cox, F. F. Bosworth, T. K. Leonard, J. Roswell Flower, S. A. Jamieson, John Sinclair, Cyrus B. Fockler, John G. Lake, J. W. Welch, and W. T. Gaston were present.

The convention opened on April 2, 1914, with preaching, prayer, and fellowship. Business began on April 6.

Bell was made the acting chairman, but the convention asked him to serve as temporary chairman for the entire convention. J. Roswell Flower was named as temporary convention secretary. The first order was to select a convention resolution committee to receive reports and proposals on pertinent subjects and to arrange them for presentation to the convention. A second committee formed and met privately out of fear that the convention would adopt a rigid structure of organization. This committee was chaired by T. K. Leonard. Its fear was unfounded, for it was soon discovered that both committees had about the same ideas. They agreed to present a preamble that set forth the principles of equality, unity, and cooperation that would govern the relationships within the association as a "voluntary cooperative fellowship," including the principle of self-governing of local churches. No constitution was adopted at the convention, and therefore for several years the preamble alone contained the guiding principles of the new organization.

The convention adopted the name The General Council of the Assemblies of God. It also approved two official periodicals: *Word and Witness*, edited by Bell, and the *Christian Evangel*, edited by Flower. It recognized the Bible school in Findlay, Ohio, and voted to make the school in Findlay its first, but temporary headquarters. Bell and Flower would publish the periodicals on the school's presses, and they would teach in the school.

The convention authorized Goss to issue credentials to those requesting such recognition in the South and West and Leonard to issue credentials to those in the North and East. A statement to deny ministerial credentials to divorced and remarried persons was adopted. The convention ended on April 12, 1914. The adopted organizational structure was little more than a name, but it had the potential of developing into a denomination with a strong central governing system.

It seemed that Pentecostals were becoming more unified, but an event occurred just three days after the Hot Springs convention that would provoke a new doctrinal controversy that would again divide Pentecostals.

After R. E. McAlister had stirred the Worldwide Apostolic Faith Camp Meeting at Arroyo Seco in the summer of 1913 by stating that the apostles had always baptized in Jesus' name rather than in the traditional trinitarian formula, both ministers and laymen began to pray for understanding and to study the Scriptures about the name of Jesus. In time Frank Ewart, Glenn Cook, and others came to accept the apostolic pattern of water baptism in the name of Jesus Christ for the remission of sins (Acts 2:38) and the apostolic teaching that in Jesus "dwelleth all the fulness of the Godhead bodily" (Colossians 2:9).

Three days after the convention in Hot Springs closed, on April 15, 1914, Frank Ewart rebaptized Glenn Cook in the name of Jesus Christ, and Cook then rebaptized Ewart in the name of Jesus Christ. This biblical act would inspire and challenge Pentecostals everywhere to follow apostolic teaching and practices, rather than merely to follow historic and traditional Christianity. Ewart and Cook's actions caused a storm of controversy and led to what their opponents would call the "New Issue."

CHAPTER FIFTEEN

THE "NEW ISSUE" AND ONENESS PENTECOSTALSM

Frank Ewart and Glenn Cook's actions on April 15, 1914, led to division within the Assemblies of God and marked the beginning of the apostolic Jesus Name Pentecostal movement that would spread throughout the world. The controversy raised by the "New Issue" would divide Pentecostals into two groups: trinitarians and Oneness believers. The struggle revealed in this story formed the foundation upon which trinitarian and Oneness Pentecostals have developed their visions, labor, practices, and place in modern Christendom.

St. Louis, Missouri

When Glenn Cook came from Los Angeles to Mother Moise's home in St. Louis in January 1915, he ignited the spark that would spread the Oneness message and Jesus Name baptism throughout the Midwest and into the South. After a week of services, Mother Moise, Mother Barnes, Ben Pemberton, and about forty others accepted the Oneness message. Although they had been baptized in the traditional formula of Father, Son, and Holy Ghost, they braved the winter wind and the icy cold waters of the Mississippi River to be rebaptized in the name of Jesus Christ.

The Assemblies of God was in the process of moving its headquarters from Findlay, Ohio, to St. Louis. Because of the need to save finances during the move, J. R. Flower, the general secretary, and E. N. Bell, the editor of the official periodicals for the Assemblies of God and who had served as its first chairman, accepted Mother Moise's invitation to use her home as a temporary headquarters.

Flower was present during the week of services, heard Cook teach on the oneness of God and Jesus Name baptism, and watched him baptize the people in the name of Jesus Christ. However, Flower, who had been brought into the Pentecostal movement under Cook's ministry in Indianapolis in 1907, rejected Cook's Oneness message.

Flower knew that Pentecostals were being baptized in the name of Jesus Christ in California from reports printed in *Meat in Due Season*, a periodical published by Frank Ewart. He probably learned that Ewart and Cook had rebaptized each other in the name of Jesus Christ in Los Angeles in April 1914, shortly after ministers in Hot Springs had created the new organization called the Assemblies of God. He also knew that this "New Issue" among Pentecostals could become as divisive as the first issue it faced over the Holiness doctrine of sanctification.

After listening to Cook and observing the baptismal service, Flower took the first step to stop the Oneness message. He wrote to G. T. Haywood, a prominent pastor of a large congregation in Indianapolis, to warn him that Cook was headed for Indianapolis with an "erroneous" doctrine.

Glen Cook baptizing L. V. Roberts in Jesus' name in Indianapolis

Indianapolis, Indiana

Arriving in Indianapolis, Cook visited both G. T. Haywood and L. V. Roberts, pastor of Oak Hill Tabernacle. At Oak Hill Tabernacle, Cook preached the Oneness message in several services, and most of the congregation soon gathered on the banks of Fall Creek to be rebaptized in Jesus' name. Cook baptized Roberts first and then his assistant pastor, Homer White, and then the rest of the congregation was rebaptized. The date was March 6, 1915.

After the Worldwide Apostolic Faith Camp Meeting at Arroyo Seco in 1913, Haywood often visited Los Angeles to discuss the issue of Jesus Name baptism that R. E. McAlister had raised during his baptismal sermon. Haywood, Cook, Ewart, and McAlister studied the Scriptures on water baptism together, but no decision had been made until early 1914 when Ewart felt the need to proclaim the full deity of Jesus Christ and how it relates to water baptism.

147

Haywood was ready to accept Cook's message in Indianapolis, but he felt that he must first share the Oneness message with his congregation. He led his congregation by having Cook baptize him in the name of Jesus Christ. After Cook baptized Haywood in Fall Creek, Haywood probably baptized approximately 469 people in his large congregation.

Cook's ministry in Indianapolis brought almost all Pentecostals in the city into the Oneness movement. More-

over, the outstanding leadership of Haywood assured that the city would remain a center of Oneness Pentecostalism.

Haywood's answer to Flower's words of warning—"Your warning came too late. I have already accepted the message and been rebaptized"—soon echoed beyond Indianapolis, for in the Midwest and South, minister after minister, mission after mission, and church after church accepted the Oneness message and were rebaptized.

G. T. Haywood

Cook's ministry in St. Louis and Indianapolis had opened the Midwest and South to the Oneness message.

The Rising Opposition

Before returning to Los Angeles, Cook stopped in St. Louis, once again staying at Mother Moise's home. This time E. N. Bell was present, and Mother Moise seated Cook at the table between Bell and Flower. Cook reported that on one day, from about 9:00 AM until late at night, he taught and discussed the Oneness message with Bell, Flower, and the staff at the home. Cook wrote that Flower's response to the apostolic pattern of Jesus Name baptism was that the apostles simply disobeyed Christ. Of course, Flower was trying to defend the traditional orthodox doctrine at the expense of good Bible exegesis, and Cook dismissed Flower's response as trivial. Cook noted, however, that Bell's response indicated that he recognized the truth of the Oneness message. Still Bell was careful in his response; he had much to lose if he accepted the Oneness message.

Cook's successful ministry in St. Louis and Indianapolis caused alarm among trinitarians in the Assemblies of God. They felt that a response was necessary to stem the growth of the "New Issue." Beginning in the March 27, 1915, issue of the *Weekly Evangel*, one of the official publications of the Assemblies of God, several articles were published against the Oneness message. In this issue Bell wrote an article entitled "Baptized Once for All." In the April 17 issue, D. W. Kerr authored an article on the trinitarian view of God. And in the May and June issues, Bell wrote several articles, including "The Sad New Issue" (June 5), to argue for the trinitarian baptismal formula. Of course, many did not the regard the "New Issue" as "sad," and the message would not stop spreading. As the Oneness message spread, trinitarians came to fear that it would become the doctrinal position of the Assemblies of God.

In a special session, the Executive Presbytery met in St. Louis on May 11 and drew up a statement in an effort to stop the Oneness message. Published in the June issue of the *Word and Witness*, the other official publication, the statement called for peace and harmony among the churches, and it clearly blamed Oneness believers for creating confusion, strife, and division. The statement attacked what it regarded as the errors of the Oneness message.

E. N. Bell Is Rebaptized

After the Executive Presbytery's statement was published in the June 1915 issue of *Word and Witness*, both Flower and Bell wrote articles in which they viewed the "New Issue" as reaching its "highwater mark" in Los Angeles and St. Louis, and indicated that it would now soon fade as other issues had. But they were wrong. The Oneness message had only begun to spread.

At the Interstate Assemblies of God Camp Meeting in Jackson, Tennessee, from July 23 to August 1, the Acts

E. N. Bell

2:38 message created another wave that spread the message rapidly throughout the Midwest and South. The host pastor, H. G. Rodgers, and E. N. Bell were to conduct the camp meeting. But after prayer, both H. G. Rodgers and E. N. Bell felt led to send a telegram to L. V. Roberts in Indianapolis, inviting him to preach at the camp: "We want your message for the camp. Take the first train."

Roberts preached his first camp sermon on Acts 2:38. To his surprise, at the end of his message, both E. N. Bell and H. G. Rodgers declared their desire to be rebaptized in the name of Jesus Christ. The baptism service was held the next afternoon. Bell was the first one rebaptized, followed by Rodgers. Hundreds of others followed them in rebaptism, and God's great glory fell upon the people. The news quickly spread, and the camp attendance grew to about 4,000 people. About seventy ministers and hundreds of laymen were baptized in the name of Jesus Christ.

News of Bell's rebaptism helped to spread the Oneness message into Arkansas, Texas, and Louisiana. At a camp meeting in Arkansas during August 1915, Bell rebaptized Howard Goss in the name of Jesus Christ. In Texas, L. C. Hall and Harvey Shearer used Bell's baptism to get ministers to consider the biblical teaching on the name of Jesus Christ in water baptism. In the August 14, 1915, issue of *Word and Witness*, Bell published his article, "Who Is Jesus Christ?" with its subheading, "Jesus Christ being rediscovered as the Jehovah of the Old Testament and the God of the New," causing many ministers to take a scriptural look at Jesus Christ being God manifested in flesh.

O. F. Fauss, a young minister attending a camp meeting in Merryville, Louisiana, during the summer of 1915, read Bell's article. He later wrote that this article caused many preachers to take a fresh look at the Scriptures. Later in December 1915, when Fauss attended the Elton Bible Conference in Louisiana, he became one of fourteen preachers who were rebaptized in the name of Jesus. Assemblies of God historian Carl Brumback reported that all twelve Assemblies of God preachers in Louisiana accepted the Oneness message.

Canada

Under the ministry of L. C. Hall, G. T. Haywood, R. E. McAlister, and Frank Small, hundreds of Pentecostals in Canada were rebaptized in the name of Jesus Christ. Again Carl Brumback stated, "With rare exceptions, most of the Canadian brethren were included in this Oneness sweep." He asked, "Where would this stop? It was becoming a veritable flood."

The Struggle within the Assemblies of God

Many of the recognized leading Pentecostal ministers embraced the Jesus Name message. In addition to Frank Ewart, Glenn Cook, G. T. Haywood, R. E. McAlister, Frank Small, Frank Bartleman, E. N. Bell, Howard Goss, and H. G. Rodgers, other leaders such as D. C. O. Opperman, A. H. Argue, George T. Studd, R. J. Scott, W. E. Booth-Clibborn, Elmer K. Fisher, L. C. Hall, Andrew D. Urshan, Harvey Shearer, Samuel McClain, B. F. Lawrence, Harry Van Loon, and many other outstanding preachers accepted the Oneness message.

Three of these leaders, Howard Goss, E. N. Bell, and D. C. O. Opperman, had been the primary promoters and organizers of the Assemblies of God. Bell served as the first chairman, Goss and Opperman served on the first board of presbyters, Goss served as the credentials committee for the western states, and Opperman was elected to be the assistant chairman at the Second General Council. B. F. Lawrence also served on the board of presbyters.

At the Third General Council of the Assemblies of God, held at Turner Hall in St. Louis on October 1-10, 1915, one day was set aside to discuss the biblical formula of water baptism. E. N. Bell and G. T. Haywood were selected to present the case for baptism in the name of Jesus Christ. A. P. Collins and William G. Schell were chosen to present the case for using the words "in the name of the Father, and of the Son, and of the Holy Ghost." When the council decided that only the Bible could be used and not church history,

Schell withdrew and Jacob Miller took his place. Each debater had thirty minutes to speak. When the four speakers finished, the issue was opened for all to discuss. This arrangement had the appearance of being fair to both views, but the next day the trinitarian council leadership allowed Schell to speak for two hours in favor of the trinitarian formula using church history.

The council passed a resolution stating that the use of a baptismal formula was not a test of fellowship. It urged ministers to end "all strife, harsh contention or division." Basically, the resolution can be viewed as being aimed at Oneness ministers since it was an attempt to halt the spread of the Oneness message. The trinitarians were also successful in eliminating all Oneness believers from leadership roles, thus gaining effective control of the organization.

During the next year, the official Assemblies of God periodicals did not publish any articles on the "New Issue," either for or against it. But the struggle to win people to one side or the other of the issue continued in the fellowship. The trinitarians won a significant victory when Bell turned from his Oneness beliefs and returned to the trinitarian group.

On October 1-10, 1916, the Fourth General Council of the Assemblies of God was held at Bethel Chapel, a small church in St. Louis. The five members selected for the resolution committee were all committed trinitarians. The trinitarian camp was now determined to make the trinitarian doctrine, including the trinitarian formula of water baptism, the official position of the Assemblies of God.

Although the published announcement for the council stated that it would be an "open" council, G. T. Haywood found it to be closed to all who were not members of the Assemblies of God. This meant that G. T. Haywood, Frank Ewart, Frank Bartleman, Glenn Cook, Harry Van Loon, and others who were not members of the Assemblies of God were not permitted to participate in the council proceedings.

On October 7, the resolution committee presented the Statement of Fundamental Truth, which required ministers to accept the doctrine of the trinity and the baptismal formula of "in the name of the Father, and of the Son, and of the Holy Ghost." With the passage of the statement, Oneness believers were forced to leave the Assemblies of God and to form another fellowship.

CONCLUSION

As stated earlier, the restoration impulse is the best lens through which to look at the rise of Pentecostalism. It was this impulse that caused early adherents to cry, "Back to Pentecost!" The influence of the restoration impulse can be seen in the self-identification of early Pentecostals as members of the Apostolic Faith movement. The Book of Acts became the hermeneutical key that unlocked a fuller understanding of Scripture.

A number of scholars have suggested that Oneness Pentecostals followed this impulse more closely. Edith Blumhofer in *Restoring the Faith: The Assemblies of God, Pentecostalism, and American Culture* wrote, "If one admits the strong restorationist component at the heart of Pentecostalism's identity, oneness Pentecostals were more zealously restorationist, more doggedly congregational, and more Christ-centered—in short, in some important ways more essentially Pentecostal—than the Trinitarians." D. William Faupel in *The Everlasting Gospel: The Significance of Eschatology in the Development of Pentecostal Thought* said, "Although the New Issue was rejected by the majority of the movement, the fact remains that it was the logical and inevitable development of Pentecostal theology."

The events of 1916 caused a significant number of Pentecostal ministers to break with the Assemblies of God in particular but with the wider trinitarian movement in general. The Oneness ministers were not long in forming their own organization. On January 2-3, 1917, the ministers formed the General Assembly of the Apostolic Assemblies. The organization was short-lived. Within a year it had merged with the Pentecostal Assemblies of the World, and on the whole, most Oneness Pentecostals were a part of this organization.

It was during the last half of this decade that Oneness Pentecostals began to develop their distinctive identity. Colossians 2:9, with its emphasis on "all the fulness of the Godhead bodily," became the key verse to understanding the full deity of Christ. The new-birth message of water and Spirit baptism was best summarized by Acts 2:38 and it became the focal point of their soteriology. The interracial impulse that was part and parcel of the Azusa Street revival was also maintained in the early years of the Oneness movement. This interracial impulse lasted almost a decade longer in the Oneness movement.

Pentecostals, especially Oneness Pentecostals, wanted to restore the church to its pristine roots. They wanted both the power and the purity of the first-century church. Oneness Pentecostals rejected the creeds of the early ecumenical councils in their attempt to replicate apostolic Christianity. Despite the fact that the so-called orthodox marginalized them, the early Oneness movement remained fervently committed to "the faith . . . once delivered unto the [church]."